LANGUAGE ACROSS THE CURRICULUM

Language Across the Curriculum

the Implementation of the Bullock Report in the Secondary School

MICHAEL MARLAND C.B.E.
Headmaster, North Westminster Community School and a member of the Bullock Committee

with specialist contributions by

Douglas Barnes

Lecturer in Education, the University of Leeds

Ann Dubs

Head of Reading Centre, Woodberry Down School

Colin Harrison and Keith Gardner

Schools Council's Effective Use of Reading Project, Nottingham University

Dr W. A. Gatherer

Chief Adviser, Lothian

Nancy Martin

Schools Council's Writing Across the Curriculum Project, University of London

Irene Robertson

Schools Council's Language Across the Curriculum (Case Studies) Project

HEINEMANN EDUCATIONAL BOOKS

Heinemann Educational Books
Halley Court, Jordan Hill, Oxford OX2 8EJ
OXFORD LONDON EDINBURGH
MELBOURNE SYDNEY AUCKLAND
SINGAPORE MADRID
IBADAN NAIROBI GABORONE HARARE
KINGSTON PORTSMOUTH NH (USA)

LCL 78 30 1577
ISBN 0 435 80631 9

First published 1977
Reprinted 1977, 1978, 1979, 1980, 1982, 1988, 1989

Printed in Great Britain by
Antony Rowe Ltd, Chippenham, Wiltshire

Contents

Acknowledgements

Although I must take full responsibility for any failings in this book, I should like to thank the many colleagues, writers, and speakers whose ideas and experiences I have found very helpful, and the members of some seventy 'Language Across the Curriculum' conferences run by schools, LEAs, and the DES which I have attended whilst writing this book, and whose questions and suggestions I have found so helpful. M.M.

Nancy Martin wishes to acknowledge with thanks: Janice Drewry, Alderman Callorn Comprehensive School; M. Torbe, Elm Bank Teachers' Centre, Coventry; D. Allen, M. Halligan, A. Macalpine, R. Minovi, Westerhope Middle School. Irene Robertson wishes similarly to thank Mr G. Steward, Headmaster, A. Hoskyns, and the fourth-year physics group of Sir William Collins School, London.

The author and publishers wish to thank the following for permission to reproduce copyright material: The *Evening Gazette* (Cleveland) for 'Continuously, monotonously . . .' by Karen Robson, pupil at Marton Sixth Form College, Middlesbrough; Longman for the diagram from *Patterns of Language* by McIntosh and Halliday; Syndication International for the leading article 'The Courage of Jack Jones' from the *Daily Mirror*; H.M.S.O. for the extracts from *A Language for Life* (The Bullock Report); Macmillan, London and Basingstoke, for the extracts from *The Development of Writing Abilities* by Britton *et al.*; Prentice-Hall, Inc., Englewood Cliffs, N.J., USA, for the diagram from p. 52 of *Be a Better Reader* Book VI, second edition, by Nila Banton Smith © 1973 by Prentice-Hall Inc.; The Schools Council and Ward Lock Educational for material quoted in connection with the Writing Across the Curriculum project in Chapter 5, pp. 145–68.

We are grateful to R. Mitson, principal of Abraham Moss Centre, Manchester, for permission to use the worksheet 'Taking Part in Discussions'. The text was produced by the Humanities team in 1974, and the illustrations are by Pete Fricker.

We would also like to thank the Headmaster of Abbey Wood School, London S.E.2., for permission to reproduce Appendix 3; the Headmaster of Culverhay School, Bath, for Appendix 5; the Working Party members for Appendix 4; Ronald Hase for considerable help towards Appendix 1.

Throughout this book, *A Language for Life*, Report of the Committee of Inquiry appointed by the Secretary of State for Education and Science under the Chairmanship of Sir Alan Bullock, F.B.A., is referred to simply as 'the Report', and that committee as 'the Committee'. All quotations from it are identified by the chapter and paragraph number in brackets immediately after the quotation.

Preface

The Heinemann Series on Organization in Schools is a systematic attempt to help schools improve the quality of the secondary-school experience by a methodical study of the ways in which they can be organized. The series has been planned to cover the central philosophy and every aspect of the planning and running of schools. Each book has been written by a different author and from a different point of view, out of his or her own observation, experience, and conviction; thus there is inevitably some overlapping between volumes, as certain topics (such as the responsibilities of senior staff, or the provision of resources) need to be included in a number of books.

Language Across the Curriculum is not a summary of the Bullock Report. I have endeavoured, with the aid of a number of specialist contributors, to take the central challenging recommendation of the report, and try to help secondary schools make it operational. Essentially, therefore, this book accepts the Report's arguments for a language policy, and takes on the task of working out some of the details. The Report gave only six pages specifically to the subject of 'language across the curriculum', although in a sense a great deal of the rest of the report was directed to that idea. Schools anxious to consider the practical implications of that central recommendation have asked for more details to consider. In this book the contributors and I endeavour to take up and expand those six pages. The scope of this book's interest means, therefore, that very many major sections of the Report are ignored completely, or referred to only from the point of view of a secondary-school language policy; there is nothing in this book about the initial stages of reading, about drama, about initial training, the provision of advisory staff, or even very much reference to many aspects of the teaching of the English Department as such.

Learning, it is now clear, involves language not merely as a passive medium for receiving instruction, but as the essential means of forming and handling central concepts. Thus learning is not merely *through* language but *with* language. The task of devising a policy adequate for this is now laid on every school. There are, however, difficulties.

In the first place the huge bulk of research, thought, and reporting on language and learning has been concerned with the early years, with 'language acquisition'. The commendable ambition of bringing secondary and primary teachers into a closer working relationship, and the obvious truth that language development goes on across such organizational divisions, has led to some overlooking of the special problems faced in the secondary age-range. Schools looking for help in formulating a language policy have found that most of the literature and most of the examples apply to the young child.

Secondly, schools have found the array of specialists somewhat bewildering. They have also found polarized philosophies, frequently over-stated in public pronouncement, which have chosen to leave out the necessary truths of other points of view.

Those of us working with secondary-age pupils have got to find a way of bringing together what is known about language with special reference to this age range, and have to synthesize the separate insights into a workable policy. Clearly no one 'policy' can be drawn up, circulated, and implemented in a diversity of schools. A policy can not be 'bought in' from some central agency. Nor, however, can it be devised in a vacuum, without the knowledge and practice that has been tried out elsewhere. This book therefore aims to provide some of the knowledge, analysis, and range of examples that will make it easier for a school to plan for its own needs. There is no blueprint policy in these pages, nor does the book pretend to give all the answers; rather it tries to list the aspects which a school might consider, and to give details of the possibilities within them.

Each of the specialist contributors has written independently, and each speaks for himself or herself. Thus they would not necessarily agree completely with each other's points, nor those of my own text. Similarly none of us would wish to claim that what we write would be entirely approved of by the Bullock Committee were it still sitting. I believe that this book is within the spirit of the report, but in working onwards from the main recommendation each of us must develop individual methods.

This book is therefore designed to be a practical help to those in secondary schools developing their own 'language policy across the curriculum', especially heads of subject departments, senior staff responsible for organizational, staffing, pastoral, curriculum, and resource decisions, heads and deputy heads, and members of the many school working parties who are trying to make sure that language and learning work together.

PART I

Towards a Whole-School Language Policy

1. The Need for a Language Policy

The bargain

138 In the secondary school, all subject teachers need to be aware of:
    (i) the linguistic processes by which their pupils acquire information and understanding, and the implications for the teacher's own use of language;
    (ii) the reading demands of their own subjects, and ways in which the pupils can be helped to meet them.

139 To bring about this understanding every secondary school should develop a policy for language across the curriculum. The responsibility for this policy should be embodied in the organizational structure of the school.

(Conclusions and Recommendations)

The central recommendation of the Bullock Report is a tough one, difficult to approach, complex to work out, and extremely taxing to implement. Yet despite its daunting challenge, comprehensive schools up and down the country have embarked upon an attempt to see what is in it for them. I have found a real enthusiasm and energy in many schools. There have been numerous conferences of representatives from schools and many one- or two-day closures when the entire staff of a school or a group of schools have come together to consider the challenge. Others have set up Working Parties or Committees to start a detailed examination of the problems of language and learning in their schools.

This vigorous reaction comes, it seems to me, from a clear realization that recommendations 138 and 139 are sound educational common sense. In a way the Committee has articulated, and supported with a careful scrutiny of a wide range of research, what experienced secondary teachers have long sensed: difficulties with language hamper understanding and growth in most areas of learning, and, conversely, those areas of learning could provide real contexts for language growth. The aim of a 'language across the curriculum policy' is simply to face that basic educational problem by endeavouring to create a 'virtuous circle': *if a school devotes thought and time to assisting language development, learning in all areas will be helped; if attention is given to language in the content and skill subjects, language development will be assisted powerfully by the context and-purpose of those subjects.* Indeed, because much of learning is possible only through the personal operation of language, unless the curriculum is planned so as to encourage a real communication and personal use of language,

3

there will be considerably less learning. If, conversely, the opportunities for pupils to explore ideas through language in the curriculum
are developed, language will grow with the learning. Thus the policy
can be seen as shrewd bargaining between teachers for the mutual
benefit of their subjects and their pupils.

The background

As the Report acknowledges, one major force in formulating ideas
for the 'language across the curriculum' movement was the work of
the London Association for the Teaching of English, a widely based
movement drawing on a larger number of practising teachers, but
centred on the Institute team, led by James (later Professor) Britton.
The Association's 1968 annual conference provided the discussion
document drafted by another member of the team, Harold Rosen,
on behalf of the Association following the work of that conference.
That document joined Douglas Barnes' now famous paper on talk
in the classroom in the book published in 1969 *Language, the Learner,
and the School*.[1] It was an influential book, important because its
concern was language, especially talk, in all learning, and because it
gave prominence to the secondary situation at a time when virtually
all language development work was orientated to the younger child.

In 1966 the Schools Council had set up the Writing Research
Team, also led by James Britton,[2] and in the revised edition of
Language, the Learner, and the School, published in 1971, Harold Rosen
included the theoretical model of discourse that the team had
developed. That year the Schools Council started a continuation
project to disseminate the findings and ideas of this research.[3] In all
that work special tribute is due to Professor Britton, whose own study
had come out the year before.[4] He represented the best of the British
tradition of academic consideration rooted in a sympathetic understanding of classroom conditions.

Of course, the British climate was favourable in many ways. Indeed
one needs to study the extraordinary separation of subject teachers
in large American high schools to realize how favourable our tradition
has been. George Sampson's famous dictum in his influential

---

[1] D. Barnes, J. Britton, H. Rosen, *Language, the Learner and the School*,
Penguin, 1970; revised edition, 1971.

[2] J. Britton, A. Burgess, N. Martin, A. McLeod, H. Rosen, *The Development of Writing Abilities 11–18*, Macmillan, Research Series, 1975.

[3] Nancy Martin's two sections, pages 145 and 231, are based on this
work.

[4] J. Britton, *Language and Learning*, Allen Lane, 1970.

English for the English ('Every teacher is a teacher of English') was widely known and quoted, even if its implications had not been properly explored. Further, the literary critics had helped by stressing the function of language. D. W. Harding had written:

> Utterances cast in the form of communication are at the same time a means of exploring one's experience and defining oneself. And they are not just a communication of the *results* of self-exploration; language processes themselves contribute to the act of discovery, leading the speaker on unexpectedly from what he intended saying to what he finds he has said.[1]

And the works of F. R. Leavis, which powerfully affected secondary school English after the war, were based on similar assumptions about the function of language.

By the end of the 'sixties the teaching of specialist English in the secondary school had been substantially if not completely rejuvenated. Despite the difficulties, confusions, and failures entailed, the new emphasis on language as a personal expression had revealed educational possibilities that would be of value outside English. The time was also propitious as psychologists, sociologists, and linguists had produced fundamental work and helpful insights that explained some at least of the difficulties educationalists were facing. Professor Britton and his team were able to synthesize these insights in the important theoretical work that provided the basis for Chapter 4 of the Report.

The Committee, as 'A unified approach' in the next chapter will make clear, drew also on an entirely different tradition, that of the students of reading. In this country reading has been thought of as something taught only to the young or the backward. In America, however, reading has long been seen as an activity that requires help and teaching, as they would say 'in the content areas'. The 'Reading Consultant' has school-wide responsibilities, and the theoretical understanding of the reading process has been developed widely. This is not surprising for, as Professor Lunzer has noted, 'Education in the USA has long been less élitist than in Britain. The teaching of "reading to learn" is an essential consequence of the democratization of Education'. The United Kingdom Reading Association worked hard to develop these ideas, and the introduction of a 'Reading Development' course in the Open University Post-Experience Course in 1972 can be taken as marking the acceptance of the need for understanding and teaching reading in the curriculum. Thus when the Bullock Committee came to consider its brief there were two strands of work available—language and learning, and reading—which related to all aspects of secondary education and were joined as the demand for a 'language across the curriculum policy'.

[1] I owe this quotation to the excellent introduction by that leader of English teachers, Denys Thompson, to his *Directions in the Teaching of English*, CUP, 1969.

Reading standards

One indication of the need for the policy is the findings of the Committee on reading needs and reading standards, and the education profession is inevitably and rightly concerned with the results of these findings. We must want to know whether we are doing the good at which we aim. Unfortunately, emotive reaction to the notion of 'standards' has made an objective consideration difficult. The Committee itself was set up at a time of national near-panic that 'standards' were declining. To some, any talk of standards is anti-educational, likely to be right-wing, anti-progressive, and élitist. However, a nation, an Authority, and an individual school must attempt to know what it is doing: it has a duty to establish its success both for educational and for financial reasons, that is to justify its mandate and to claim its funding. As we move towards a closer relationship with our local communities, indeed, we are likely to be held even more accountable, and now the expansionist and optimistic years are over, the call to reveal and explain is likely to be stronger than ever. We have barely started to evaluate, but we must, and a book in this series will be devoted to assisting schools with their own evaluation.[1]

The Report studied very carefully the available data on reading standards, mainly the NFER surveys of 1948 through to 1971. Chapter Two of the Report explores in detail the reasons why, contrary to public expectation, it is not possible to agree that standards in the early 'seventies were lower than earlier. In the first place there was considerable doubt about the statistical basis of the testing in 1971, and more significantly there was strong criticism of the validity of the tests, which had dated badly. A simple statistical point needs explanation: as standards *overall* increased in the post-war years, the mean naturally rose. As the test used remained the same, the tested population moved up towards the highest possible scores in the test, the 'ceiling' thus coming nearer to the mean. The more able fifteen-year-olds were by then already performing so well that they were unable to improve their scores: they had hit the 'ceiling'. This meant that the computed mean could no longer rise with the rising standards, as the superior scores, artificially held back, depressed the true mean. As the Report commented: 'Reading ability has outstripped the available tests' (2.34).

However, for secondary schools some of the findings on standards are important, provided that one remembers that these are national averages, and there are substantial local variations. The following conclusions are the relevant ones:

[1] Martin Shipman, *In-School Evaluation*, Heinemann Organization in Schools Series, forthcoming.

Definitions of the terms 'literate' and 'illiterate' vary to so great an extent as to make them of little value as currently employed. (2.1–2.2)
The level of reading skill required for participation in the affairs of modern society is far above that implied in earlier definitions of literacy. (2.2)
Comparability of levels of 'literacy' between countries is difficult to determine. However, there is no evidence that standards in England are lower than those of other developed countries. (2.3)
There is no firm statistical base for comparison of present-day standards of reading with those of before the war; and in terms of today's problems it is questionable whether there is anything to be gained from attempting it. (2.11)
The tests at present in use in national surveys are inadequate measures of reading ability, since they measure only a narrow aspect of silent comprehension. (2.13)
The changes in the last decade in the scores of 15-year-olds on both tests are not statistically significant, and standards in this age group remained the same over the period 1960/71. In the light of the limitations of the tests this fact is not in itself disturbing. (2.19)
There is no evidence of a decline in attainment over the years in the lowest achievers among 15-year-olds. Since national surveys were instituted in 1948 the standards of the poorest readers have risen, and the gap between the most able and least able has narrowed. This reflects upon the capacity of existing tests to measure the achievement of the most able readers. (2.19; 2.29)
There was no significant change in the reading standards of 11-year-olds over the decade 1960–1970, but such movement as took place after 1964 was in all probability slightly downwards. (2.20; 2.29)
There is evidence to suggest that this probable slight decline in the scores of 11-year-olds may well be linked to a rising proportion of poor readers among the children of unskilled and semi-skilled workers. (2.22–2.25; 2.29)
There is some evidence that children of seven are not as advanced as formerly in those aspects of reading ability which are measured by tests. (2.26–2.28)

Some of these points are worth pondering:
1. The evidence does support concern at possible lower reading standards at eleven, and research subsequently published from the ILEA literacy survey confirms this.[1] That the fall has been pulled up by the age of fifteen as far as one can see should not be allowed to mask the fact that the secondary experience is thus diminished by the reading deficiency of the pupil during those years.
2. The composition of the group who are less able readers has changed. It is now more homogeneously working-class. This depressing fact was not noticed in press coverage, and has such implications, after a quarter of a century of egalitarian education, that it is worth emphasizing here. The report found:

> While reading standards at the lower end of the ability range have improved in most socio-economic groups, the poor readers among the

[1] ILEA, Research and Statistics.

children of the unskilled and semi-skilled have not improved their standards commensurately. The result is that the lower end of the ability range has an increased proportion of these children. (2.25)

Although we can be encouraged by the closing of the gap between the most and least able, and the overall improvement of the least able, we must surely be deeply concerned by this fact.
3. Whatever the overall effects, standards are not good enough for current cultural and social needs:

> It is obvious that as society becomes more complex and makes higher demands in awareness and understanding of its members the criteria of literacy will rise. (2.2)

There is clearly no room for complacency, but a real need for strenuous effort. The effort required must be across the whole curriculum if it is to be effective.

Whole-school policies

This central idea is being considered at a suitable time, for, it seems to me, now that comprehensive schools have been established almost throughout the country, the first requirements of their establishment have been met, and the new organism is being evaluated and re-shaped. The great strength of the comprehensive school is variety— of pupils, families, staff, and learning activities. This variety is an exciting, heady educational brew, but it should not be allowed to disguise the crucial danger of the comprehensive school, which is the corollary of its variety: fragmentation. The sections of the school pull apart too easily, each looking inward to its own development and each Department becoming a separate power structure, offering pupils a separate unrelated experience. At the same time others in the school, overawed by the intense build-up of teacher talent and committed expertise in various areas, pull back to their own specialism, leaving language to the English teachers. An Art Department becomes a centre of visual stimulus whilst the rest of the school is a visual desert;[1] the English Department becomes the 'sensitive centre of feeling and expression'; the craft department the only area where workmanship is admired, and so on. This tendency towards fragmentation is often more noticeable to the careful visitor than to the permanent member of staff, who has learnt to take it for granted. In these schools there is little dialogue across the school, meetings

[1] cf. The description of the Art Department in *The Creighton Report* by Hunter Davies, Hamish Hamilton, 1976.

are only in Departmental teams, and the pupil is on a package tour from subject to subject.

In facing this degree of fragmentation, it is important to see that so-called 'integration' is not necessarily a solution, indeed my observation is that whatever merits there may be in bringing a group of subjects together,[1] fragmentation, far from being overcome, is actually often made more intense: some of the fragments will have become larger and internally more coherent, but the isolation between them may be even greater. The Humanities faculty may be sharply cut off from the Creative Arts faculty, even more than used to be the case with a gaggle of small Departments in a crowded staff room.

If the strength of the comprehensive school is variety, the challenge is to avoid fragmentation, retain that variety, and achieve coherence. Coherence in a school does not necessarily mean integrated areas; it certainly does not mean that every, or even some, parts of the work should be moulded to feel the same, so that Housecraft, social studies, and English are interchangeable. It means instead that, whilst each aspect of work in the comprehensive school should be encouraged to be different, to retain its special contribution, there should be properly worked out agreements amongst the staff on a number of 'whole-school policies'. There would be agreements on overall aims, and a precise understanding of what is contributed by all and what is contributed by certain specialisms. For these agreements I prefer the phrase 'whole-school policies' for the obvious but important reason that the *whole* school, including its pastoral work, central approaches to pupils, and relations with parents, must be involved.

There are a number of important aims for whole-school policies: moral education, preparation for work, visual literacy, and social education are among them. The theme of this book is that in achieving coherence whilst retaining variety, the building of a whole-school language policy could be the most important and the most valuable.

Disseminated and specialized approaches

In considering whole-school policies, I find it helpful to think of two approaches to the curriculum, that is two approaches to helping pupils learn any desired skill or aspect of knowledge. It is possible to consider any of our curriculum aims against these two approaches:

(a) *Disseminated*. This approach argues that a particular activity is too important to be left to specialists. To leave it to a timetabled slot

[1] I discuss the grouping of learning activities in detail in *The Curriculum and Timetable of the Secondary School*, forthcoming in this series.

would be to risk artificial isolation. 'We must all join in!' is the battle cry. Thus a Head teacher may say 'Preparation for work is too important to be limited to a specialist "careers" lesson. It permeates our curriculum, so that we all contribute'.

(b) *Specialized*. The opposite approach fears that if specific provision with a specialist at a fixed time is not made, the aspect under consideration will at best be mishandled by under-prepared teachers, and at worst disappear altogether. A Head teacher of this persuasion will declare 'Preparation for work is too important to be left to anyone when he or she feels like it. We make sure it's properly taught by teachers who've got some knowledge and training'.

The pros and cons of both the disseminated and the specialized approaches are clear:

Disseminated	*Specialized*
possibility of linking to other concerns	risk isolation
pupils sense importance through variety of staff involved	pupils sense importance through focus of staff involved
risk of no one having sufficient expertise and experience	security of known specialists
risk of activity being ignored	certainty of pupils meeting 'proper' tuition

It is interesting to see where a school stands on any aspect of the curriculum:

Moral Education usually Disseminated, but not always. The Schools Council's Moral Education Project is often used as specialized material.

Sexual Education specialized

Careers usually specialized, though I argue for disseminated

—and so on. Careful curriculum planning involves judging which combination of these two approaches suits the aim. A whole-school language policy is likely to demand *both* approaches.

The diagram attempts to show the activities a school might encourage its pupils to engage in. The vertical axis indicates any subject, with pure exposition and exercise at the top. As you move *down* the subject axis, you move to learning situations in which there is a demand for pupil activity: projects, practical group-work, visits, etc. Similarly, the horizontal axis indicates pure language work, with sheer de-contextualized instruction at the farthest point, and language used in an activity on the left. At the extremes, language and subjects are far away from each other, neither bearing on each other. In the

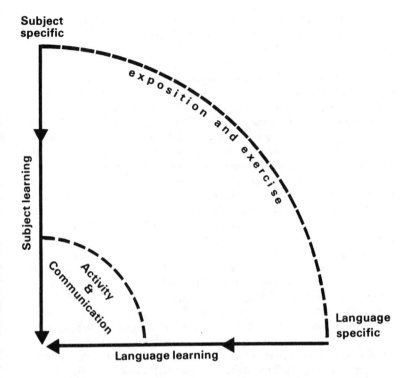

centre they converge, and it becomes impossible to divide subject from language, for the two are fused in the activity. It is here that the most valuable learning probably takes place, but the experience must include the ends of each line; a pupil will not usually make the centre without the experience of the ends.

Teaching and using language

The ultimate aim is always use. Understanding normally comes best when use is possible. We know now from extensive research that learning *about* language rarely improves *use* of language. However, we cannot learn merely by use without reflection, explanation, and theorizing.

It has been well said by the American Harold L. Herber, who has carefully analysed the relationship between the specific teaching and the *use* of skills: 'Independence should be looked upon, not as a means, but as the end product of skills and content instruction'.[1] He goes on to make the basic point that those who wish for independent

[1] Harold L. Herber, *Teaching Reading in Content Areas*, Prentice-Hall, 1970, p. 30.

learning should consider the idea that: 'If independent activity is expected and students have not been *shown how* to perform that activity, this is *assumptive* teaching.'[1] I draw the conclusion that specific preparation for independent learning is always required, both in short straightforward assignments like a reading homework and in lengthy sequences like a project activity. This preparation is best offered in two forms: specifically in isolation, and taught simultaneously within the context of other subjects.

Assumptive teaching *assumes* that skills have already been mastered, or will grow in the course of the activity. There is a tendency to push the assumptive teaching lower and lower down the•age groups as teachers of each year-group progressively consider that the best preparation for the independence of the following year is independence *this* year also. A whole-school policy in any field would never assume such mastery of skills. It would analyse the skills and knowledge required, endeavour to establish how they are best acquired and developed, and plan contexts and activities so that they provided the best opportunities for practice and use, with the necessary specific teaching when required. In a whole-school policy the link would not be left to chance, but would be articulated in a policy document, and carried out by the teacher in the activity context when teaching occurs at the precise point of need, according to the policy, and drawing on the shared knowledge.

For a fully coherent curriculum policy, two approaches must be closely interrelated. The entire teaching staff must know that specific tuition is given in certain skills by known teachers and at agreed stages. And all those giving specific tuition must know that context and purpose will be created in a variety of other situations by their colleagues, and that these situations will call on the pupils' memories of the specific teaching. One without the other, or both without an overall plan, is to leave the learning to chance or to restrict it to isolated exercises.

Using language

I sometimes think of the secondary school and its work as a complex organization to *increase* the differentiation in language skills. Those who come to us weak are increasingly offered less stretching challenges (especially when we have multi-task mixed-ability groups) and are allowed in all subjects to find ways around language difficulties. They may in mid-schooling then opt for the strikingly less language-orientated subjects. Thus they arrive weak, and go out

[1] ibid.

hardly any more experienced, whilst the more linguistically able are constantly confronted with language demands and with experiences that generate further language development. The two extremes pull farther apart.

Within the classroom there is a similar process. This results from the ingenuity of many teachers in by-passing language. We circumnavigate print, we reduce writing to gap-filling, we cut down teacher talk, and we lower our expectation of pupil talk. Half knowledge about socio-linguistics, and myths about the class bias of language encourage this further. In a misguided attempt to take pupils 'direct' to knowledge and skills, without losing them in a fog of verbal problems, we dramatically reduce their opportunity to develop language, and deny them the greatest tool to knowledge. At its simplest the pedagogical question at the heart of this book is whether to *use* language or avoid it. What does the teacher do when a pupil baulks at a language situation? That is the core of a language across the curriculum policy. Those who help him *round* it, will also cut down the number and importance of such situations. Those who would help him *through* it would also wish to plan those language situations carefully. All teachers need to be concerned about pupils' use of language. While pupils having difficulty with language must have the unhampered opportunity to flourish in those subjects in which reading and writing play a lesser part, the teachers of those subjects still have a language responsibility. It is unfair to ask the English teachers to carry the entire burden, bad psychology to encourage the pupils to think that good writing matters only in English, and a pity to miss the opportunity to help pupils learn language use in other contexts.

Building a whole-school language policy will help all members of staff devise suitable language situations and indicate strategies to help them through those situations. Some of these, no doubt the easier to agree upon, will be small technicalities, useful common approaches to skills. Such details must not be seen as beneath our linguistic ambitions. On the other hand a policy will never be built merely on such details.

If we are to lead the pupils *into* language, and not devote our ingenuity to helping them *around* it, we must consider the language very carefully. Thus a language policy will be partly concerned with what kind of language we use to explore our subjects, what kind of reading material we offer, and what kind of writing we expect from the pupils. We should not avoid using language, but we should ensure that for the pupil it is usable language that we offer.

True use of language requires something to be expressed, a context, and an audience—someone whose response matters to the writer or speaker. These conditions are simple enough to understand, but difficult to create in mass education. The 'exercise' is very nearly at the opposite extreme: it consumes words without allowing the essential ingredients of a language context. 'Correction' similarly denies the pupil the essential function of a responsive audience, offering only an error filter. Yet the school situation is not as gloomy as that may suggest. The heart of a whole-school language policy is finding and cherishing 'language contexts'. This can be done, and not only by the laborious devising of unusual schemes involving elaborate planning. Indeed it could be argued that only if the 'exercises' in 'the classes' can be converted to fill this need is there any hope for a language policy, for in schools we work in and with groups.

2. The Bullock Report and the Policy

The Bullock Report considered, in relation to schools:

(a) all aspects of teaching the use of English, including reading, writing, and speech;

(b) how present practice might be improved and the role that initial and in-service training might play;

(c) to what extent arrangements for monitoring the general level of attainment in these skills can be introduced or improved;

(page xxxi)

For the purposes of the secondary-school language policy, it is important to sense what kind of report it is, and to see how it bears on our concerns. In this section I shall highlight eight *aspects* of the report which seem to me to help focus our concerns. These are not specific recommendations from Bullock, but are themes which run through the Report, and which bear centrally on the idea of a whole-school language policy.

The importance of language

It has become a fashionable half-truth to declare that we live in a visual age, that with the dominance of the visual image and its cheap availability in newspaper, magazine, hoarding, and screen, the word has become less important, virtually a thing of the past. Such arguments point to the vividness of the news photographs, the way advertising communicates most of its message by a picture, the diagram which so effectively replaces written instructions, the flow-chart and pictogram, even the international wordless toilet signs throughout the world. Half-remembered extracts from Marshall Macluhan confirm this version of reality. Even if the word is still admitted as useful, so this argument goes, it is virtually only the spoken word, for the telephone, the radio, and the television have replaced writing and reading for all but a few specialists. For too long schools have concentrated remorselessly on the archaic and alien (i.e. exclusively middle-class) culture of print. We have not prepared people for the aural world of spoken communication, so vital in an economy of service industries and personal communication.

There is much truth in this argument. However, it gets the elements wrong; it confuses the relationship between the uses of language; and it oversimplifies the relationship between education and subsequent skills.

The truth is that communication media are in competition with each other to only a limited extent. It is perfectly possible for there to have been the expansion in visual and spoken communication without the written word declining. The evidence in fact shows clearly that the use of the written word has increased. As society has changed and the manufacturing and mining industries have given way to various forms of 'service' industry the written word has become considerably more important:

> The changing pattern of employment is making more widespread demands on reading and writing skills and therefore exposing deficiencies that may have escaped attention in the past. (1.2)

This is true across most of the employment ranges. The manager of a group of National Health Service dental clinics, for instance, has told me of the horror the recruits have of the desk, because it involves paperwork, where young employees find difficulties. In higher, but still widespread job levels the demands are greater:

> The expansion in Junior Management has been considerable, and one dimension of competence at this level is the ability to produce a written report. (1.2)

Of course a considerably larger proportion of an age group aim for Further or Higher Education after school, and even in the most practical or vocationally orientated courses, print remains a substantial, indeed the dominant, source of learning. It shows no signs of reducing, and every sign of increasing.

Outside education and employment the ordinary demands of life still expect an easy ability to cope with print. The simplest daily newspaper requires a reading age of thirteen for a reasonable level of comprehension. My experience of recent class teaching is that very many older secondary pupils cannot get much of the sense from most sections of a newspaper. The editorial of *The Sun* or the *Daily Mirror* is really baffling to many. As we offer more participation to a wider spectrum of society, print-needs increase. Even claiming one's rights and finding one's way around society require the ability to read. The Report noted that 34 per cent of Americans tested in a 1971 survey by the US National Reading Council were unable to read an application for medical aid. There is no doubt that in reading alone 'the level required for participation in the affairs of modern society is far above that implied in earlier definitions. It is obvious that as society becomes more complex and makes higher demands in awareness and understanding of its members the criteria of literacy will rise' (2.2). This is true also beyond reading. Whilst it may be true that the telephone has decreased the amount of letter writing amongst those who were likely to have been the frequent and lengthy letter writers of previous eras, the need to put pen to paper has become greater across the population as a whole. The rise in the importance of speech is similarly frequently misunderstood. We have moved away from the oral tradition, and now the purposes for which speech is required and the mode necessary for many of these purposes seems to me to require the sustenance of a wider literacy. There is no returning to the oral tradition of rural areas, nor is it honest to claim that the average person today feels at ease with fluent speech if he or she cannot read and write to a similar level of competence.

Language, thought, and learning

If literacy in its widest sense is necessary for modern society, it is also necessary for the educational process that lasts until pupils are sixteen, or in many cases seventeen or eighteen. As the report comments: 'The one feature shared by all educational institutions is that they make heavy demands on the language of those who learn and those who teach'. It is curious that we have worked so vigorously on the great post-war dream of secondary education for all without realizing that it requires the underpinning of literacy: 'The success of the secondary school can be said to depend very considerably on the level of achievement in reading and language. Unless the pupil can read, write, and talk competently he cannot benefit from the range of learning which the secondary school provides' (15.31). Curiously many of the movements in secondary education require more reading, or if not more quantitively, the reading is more important: Nuffield Science, SMP Maths, the Humanities Curriculum Project, and much that is now the commonplace of the Crafts and the Humanities. As 'chalk and talk' has been replaced by source materials, worksheets, topic books, resource-based learning, and the extensive use of libraries, literacy has been made functionally essential to education, especially with older pupils. Even a teacher intending to place discussion work at the focus of the attention finds that for all except a few contribution to the discussion is severely limited by literacy problems. The non-reader who can talk really coherently will be found, but is rare in our society and especially in our schools. Language is vital to learning to provide access to the source materials and the learning experiences.

This dependence of schooling on language is no mere useless stumbling block put in the way of the young as self-protection by the middle-class, middle-aged, formally educated. It can be shown, as Dr Gatherer points out in the next chapter, that the process of thought itself is dependent on language, and growth in the first depends on growth in the second. It is by verbalizing experiences that a young person can generalize them, and thus 'work on' them. Only through language can we hypothesize, and the ability to hypothesize is the central ability of developed thought:

> The effort to formulate a hypothesis, to put into words some possibility we have envisaged, results in a 'spelling out' to which we may then return, in the light of further experience and in search of further possibilities. By a kind of spiral, the formulation itself becomes a source from which we draw further questions, fresh hypotheses. The statement we have made becomes an object of our own contemplation and a spur to further thinking. It is probably true to say that *the higher* thought processes become possible to the child or adolescent who in this way learns to turn his linguistic activities back upon his own formulations. (4.7)

Professor Jerome Bruner sees the development of analytic thinking as one of the major contributions of secondary schooling, but he stresses that it is through strenuous pressure on language development that this capacity is gained:[1]

> What is significant about the growth of mind in the child is to what degree it depends not upon capacity but upon the unlocking of capacity by techniques that come from exposure to the specialized environment of culture[2]

The report sees language not merely as a dressing for thought, a way of making previously achieved knowledge clear. It sees the process of thinking as part of the process of developing language, and, again, the virtuous circle needs to be set up by the teacher so that the one helps the other. The two sides to this are illustrated in these two points:

> Language has a heuristic function: that is to say a child can learn by talking and writing as certainly as he can by listening and reading. To exploit the process of discovery through language in all uses is the surest way of enabling a child to master his mother tongue. (4.10)

Thus language helps learning and learning helps language, and the more closely the two are related the more effective the total process.

Reading and language

There is a tendency in schools to think of reading as a separate activity, requiring separate tuition. Indeed, as the setting up of the

---

[1] cf. 'Language as an Instrument of Thought', in A. Davies (ed.), *Problems of Language and Learning*, Heinemann Educational Books, 1975.

[2] J. S. Bruner, *The Course of Cognitive Growth* (1964), reprinted in A. Cashadan, *et al.*, *Language in Education*, Routledge & Kegan Paul, for the Open University Press, 1972, p. 166.

Committee was accompanied by public speculation about a possible decline in 'reading standards', the Committee was labelled by many as 'the reading committee'. From the first, however, it was clear to members that this was an unhelpful limitation: it is impossible to consider reading as an isolated educational activity.

On the one hand, ability to read depends on and grows out of language ability. Indeed, reading of a passage that is too far beyond the reader's verbal experience is virtually impossible. As reading is *not* simply a matter of decoding word by word in left-to-right sequence, but of a continuous speculation and checking, if a reader has to spend too long on an individual word, he loses the overall sense. Similarly, the guessing ahead is eased if the reader is familiar with many of the word collocations. On the other hand, writing and talking skills grow out of reading. Not only are individual words picked up from the 'passive' skills of reading (and listening), but whole possibilities of how words can be put together are absorbed, ready to be called on in the 'active' uses.

Some language skills are patently common to all uses. For instance, one of the highest and most difficult language skills is the ability to *reorganize* information. A good reader, like a good writer or a good speaker, has to be able to absorb a sequence of points, and re-create these to meet a specific need. The reader who can take the points made only in the order in which they are given, is limited in the same way as the writer who can list his points only in narrative order.

Thus although, as I shall discuss later, *specific* attention to reading is also required, a major theme of the report is the importance of conceiving the reading curriculum as an interwoven part of the total language curriculum.

The continuity of reading

If my last point can be thought of as 'horizontal', that is that learning to read takes its place across a variety of activities, there is an even less well understood point to be stressed which could be called vertical: learning to read, and thus being taught to read, takes place in all years of the secondary school. The Report quotes a simple but telling axiom of I. A. Richards: 'We are all of us learning to read all the time'. The Report sees the teaching of reading as a continuous process, certainly throughout the years of the secondary school.

Popular phraseology, even that in use amongst teachers, encourages a 'threshold' view of reading: 'Can he read yet?' 'He's learnt to read.' 'Do you have many non-readers?' These and similar phrases only too clearly suggest there is a single step called 'learning to read'; it is easily identified; and when reached, well, that's that, and we can all sigh with relief. Parents have the greatest temptation to view learning to read in this episodic way—one of the childhood milestones that it is a mercy to be able to stop worrying about because there's change of school and all that adolescent turbulence ahead. But teachers fall into the over-simplification also; many teachers of older junior pupils too readily expect their pupils to be able to read, and certainly most secondary teachers expect it of all their pupils, identifying 'backward readers' who fall below a certain criterion. This label gains the pupils the help of a remedial teacher, but it also allows the rest of us to leave the teaching of reading to those teachers. They handle the 'non-readers' and therefore know about teaching reading, while we handle the 'readers' (although some seem a trifle ropey), and obviously there's no need for us to know about how to teach reading. This is to commit two related fallacies:

1. *The fallacy of the threshold*, which presumes a clear cut-off between reading and not reading. Even if certain tests at certain times arbitrarily define a certain standard as the threshold below which a pupil is a 'non-reader', in practice we know that there is an infinite gradation from the first recognition of the meaningful shapes of letters to the complex ability of an educated adult to be able to reconstruct the author's intentions from the printed page. Certainly there are moments on that gradation that are especially significant: the first de-coding of a word; achieving a reading age of nine; and the age of thirteen is also perhaps an important threshold, marking the start of the ability to cope with a free range of self-chosen unedited texts. There is probably, it seems to me, an unmeasured step, not reached by many, which allows free access to the bulk of complex adult prose. Despite these rough stages, it is important to realize that pupils need help with their basic primary skills in reading well beyond these early thresholds, and there is no huge single step called 'learning to read'.

2. *The fallacy of basic skills*. The attitude that learning to read, once done, can be left behind, fails to recognize that word recognition is merely the primary skill, inadequate on its own. There is a hierarchy of reading skills, through the intermediate skills of sequences of words, to the comprehension skills. When it can be shown that as many as one third of the adult population cannot adequately comprehend popular news items and the like, it is easy to accept the arguments for the teaching of reading continued beyond word recognition to the real grappling with the sense. Too many of us— indeed most of the nation's secondary teachers—have presumed that once word recognition was roughly mastered all else would follow, that basic skills *were* 'reading'.

The report thus suggests a thread of reading tuition (discussed in Chapter 5) stretching from the earliest years to the end of formal education, *for all pupils*. It is worth knowing in the secondary school that the Report also pushes this back to the earliest stages. Whilst it accepts the concept of 'reading readiness', it substantially modifies the passive acceptance of this:

> It cannot be emphasised too strongly that the teacher has to help the children towards readiness to read. There is no question of waiting for readiness to occur; for with many children it does not come 'naturally' and must be brought about by the teacher's positive measures to induce it. (7.11)

Not only are the beginnings to be thus pushed back, but considerable encouragement is given to achieving satisfactory skills by the time of change from first or Junior schools. Although no fixed levels can be given for any age it is vital to keep the encouragement going:

> Delay beyond the age of seven in beginning to read puts a child at educational risk. There is evidence to show that many children who have made little progress in reading on entering the junior school are even further behind at eleven and that this deficiency continues to the end of their statutory school life. (Conclusions & Recommendations 212, 18.4)

The thread, though, continues right through the secondary stage, for there will be some pupils still needing substantial help with word recognition skills during these years; almost all the pupils will also need help when facing a new word or a sentence with a teasing word order. Immediately it is agreed that 'basic skills' are not mastered once and for all, it is obvious that every secondary teacher must be able and willing to give help at basic skills. It also means that the intermediate and higher skills *need teaching*.

The corollary of this is that the hierarchy of reading skills should not be thought of as something through which the pupil passes, leaving earlier stages behind. *Teaching must be available for all stages simultaneously.* Thus the seven-year-old should be faced with inference, reorganization, evaluation, and appreciation, much as word recognition, word attack skills, and the intermediate skills of sentence construing should not be thought of as left behind in the secondary school:

> The development of reading skills is a progressive one, and there are no staging points to which one can attach any particular ages. We cannot therefore speak of kinds of reading ability as being specific to the middle years and as something essentially different from those used in the upper forms of the secondary school. The primary skills of the early years mature into the understanding of word structure and spelling patterns. The intermediate skills, so essential in word attack in the early stages, are at work in skimming, scanning, and the extraction of meaning in the more complex reading tasks of the later stages. The comprehension skills themselves do not change; it is in the increasing complexity of the purpose to which they are put as the pupils grow older that the difference lies. (8.1)

If 'we are all of us learning to read all the time', and if we accept that pupils in the secondary school, of all abilities and all ages, have a range of reading difficulties, then those of us working in secondary schools must 'all of us be teaching reading all the time' also.

The need for intervention

In all work with language there is a tension, which can be creative, between two approaches, the contextual and the didactic. (These models are analogous to the disseminated and the specialized approaches to the curriculum, which I outlined in general terms on pages 9–11.) The first quite rightly stresses the need to create interest in the pupil, to motivate by an end product, and to offer stimulus and encouragement. It hopes that the skills will be *required* by the context and thus that the need to learn them will engender the actual learning. The second quite rightly stresses the importance of actually explaining things, on giving practice in skills, of 'teaching'. Contextual learning suggests that specific tuition will be meaningless without purpose and context. Didactic learning fears that without clear explanation the context will be insufficient to give real learning opportunities.

In practice, no teacher has a strategy which entirely ignores one or the other. In theory many teachers, however, do over-stress one or the other, fashionably the contextual. The Report holds a careful balance between the two, recognizing essentially that *purpose* is required for language growth, and therefore that the teacher must always look for ways of creating contexts, but also that *intervention* is essential. I should say, therefore, that it is an interventionist report. This conclusion indicates the balance: 'Language competence grows incrementally, through an interaction of writing, talk, reading, and experience, and the best teaching deliberately influences the nature and quality of this growth' (C & R 3). This 'deliberate influence' is more specifically defined elsewhere as intervention, and the balance is carefully put:

> The handling of language is a complex ability, and one that will not be developed simply by working through a series of textbook exercises. If we regard this approach as inadequate we have equal lack of sympathy with the notion that forms of language can be left to look after themselves. On the contrary, *we believe the teacher should intervene, should constantly be looking for opportunities to improve the quality of the utterance.* (1.10)

My italics there point the theme of this book: to help a school find ways in which all its teachers can intervene positively, but within a real language context.

There is a growing body of thought that it is precisely the less favoured pupils who require the most, but also the most careful, intervention. Douglas Pidgeon, for instance, has argued[1] persuasively that in the initial stages of reading it is children who have not experienced in their homes the 'specific expectancies of what reading was going to be like, of what the activity consisted of, of the purpose and use of it' who need pre-reading help with phonics before word recognition is possible. Those experienced in teaching less able secondary-age pupils similarly find that more help must be given, more specific intervention is necessary. It is important to stress, however, that there is no suggestion that the less favoured children do not require a rich context in which to use language. Of course, they do, but this will be insufficient without appropriate intervention. In his anxiety not to be over-dominant and in his wish to allow the pupil the opportunity for self-motivated growth, the teacher must not slip into the opposite failure, which is 'assumptive teaching'— assuming that points are understood.

A variety of solutions

A consistent theme of the Report is that there is no single, simple, magic solution to any aspect of language education. This conclusion was not arrived at lightly. It did not please the journalists, who would undoubtedly have preferred a strong recommendation for this that or the other 'technique', nor some of the witnesses who gave their evidence—for some were pushing single solutions. The hope of agreeing that some method of organizational approach would offer certainty of success probably lay in many people's minds. The Report found that each teaching situation requires a different combination of approaches. Thus, on the initial stages of learning to read: 'There is no one method, medium, approach, device, or philosophy that holds the key to the process of learning to read' (C & R 56), and a similar refusal to offer 'the key' will be found in the sections on curriculum organization (15.3–15.4) and pupil grouping (15.10–15.11).

A careful questioning of the experts, who appeared at first to be overwhelmingly stressing one approach, revealed that their own convictions were not in fact overwhelming: the self-styled National Council for Educational Standards did not in fact recommend a full diet of clause analysis, nor did the proponents of an 'imaginative, creative' approach actually imply that there should be no specialized technical teaching. Time and again it became clear that although popular educational articles and talks tend to peddle polarities, a

[1] Douglas Pidgeon, *Logical Steps in the Process of Learning to Read*, Educational Research, Volume 18, Number 3, NFER, June, 1976.

careful observation of actual teaching and research reveals no support for the extreme positions. It seems that it is not the system that matters, but being systematic; it is not the method that matters, but being methodical. Indeed it is one of the hard facts of educational decision-making that when a decision is made to choose one course or another it is important to realize that there is some virtue in the course rejected, and a compensation has to be built into the decision for that which has been lost.

There is no place for superficial polarities, presuming that the truth of one point of view means there is no truth in another. This is specially so of the pseudo-polarities of 'progressive' and 'traditional'. Neville Bennett's now famous research[1] followed the Report, and despite its inevitable limitations of methodological completeness in measuring language, showed in detail that primary teaching cannot always be so divided. My own review of the studies of language in the secondary school lead me to stress that success in most of the supposedly 'progressive' aims involves a marked 'traditional' component. This is especially true of independent study, the use of multiple learning sources, and of the pupil's ability to question and think for himself.

From the point of view of a secondary pupil's language development, it is clear that there is no single policy that will provide the magic solution. Neither a teaching method, an organizational procedure, nor a particular line in learning materials will itself make a sufficiently strong impact. In rejecting the efficacy of any method in itself, the Committee was not endeavouring to compromise—it is the *easy* way out in educational discussion to plump for one 'method' as totally hopeful, and the Committee chose the harder course. It came to realize that the *total* pattern of the educational process needs attention. The ingredients must be right, but the overall pattern cannot be left to tradition or chance.

School management

This central recommendation of the Report has major implications for school management. Indeed the Report is deeply concerned with overall school management, for only if the whole school can be mobilized is there a possibility of a substantial move forward. The first decade of comprehensive schools developed through the power and intensity of their subject departments. It was in these teams, vigorously led and finding new strength from the number of specialists brought together, that the curriculum was extended. But it was extended patchily, and in a disconnected way. Indeed the

[1] Neville Bennett, *Teaching Styles and Pupil Progress*, Open Books, 1976.

force towards 'Integration' was a reaction to this divisiveness. I argue elsewhere[1] that this is not the only or the necessary reaction to the less happy effects of Departmental strength and separateness. One essential series of strands in this coherence is whole-school curriculum policies. These are the deliberate planning of curriculum aims that are to be achieved not merely via one subject or range of activity, but in a number, or indeed all. This way of looking at the curriculum implies that there is central planning in the school, and that this central planning can cope with detail. For the sake of this discussion the mode of such planning is not important. Whether it is fully democratic, centred in one person, or uses some combination of approaches, is not vital to the point that coherence is possible only if there is central oversight and control. Implementation of the Report requires an overall agreement and central oversight and control in the school. It must be agreed and published what specific teaching is given on all aspects of language. Then all teachers must agree on the complementary approaches that they will use. In its support of this view, the report can be seen as a treatise on school management: to be concerned about literacy is to be concerned about school management.

A unified approach

Above all it is a unified report. Too much of the writing about aspects of English teaching throughout the 'fifties and 'sixties was fragmentary. That was the period of 'English through this' and 'English through that'. It was the period of polarities, when creativity became set against accuracy, and the imagination against technical control. Those working in linguistics were felt to be in a different camp to those educated in literature. The teaching of reading was seen as a technicality quite separate from imaginative response to literature. English specialists vied with each other, and departments within schools were often engaged in internecine disputes, or if the department was unified then it was as likely to be at odds with the school, claiming a sensitivity and responsiveness to pupil needs beyond the rest of the staff. Astoundingly good work was done in patches, but at the price of overlooking the entire range of language needs of a pupil, and at the expense of failing to mobilize the total strength of a school.

The journals, the records of conferences, teachers' books, and pupils' books all stand witness to this fragmentation, in which the passion of adherents to an approach drove teachers with a different emphasis to feel that they were in conflict. This split was seen at its strongest

[1] *Comprehensive Schools*, forthcoming in this series.

in the United States, where the teachers of 'English' felt themselves to be in a virtually different profession to the teachers of 'Reading'. Indeed they belonged to different professional associations, with little in common. As the separate teaching of reading has continued right through the High School years, the two professions confront each other in a way which is avoided by the tapering off of the separate (remedial) teaching of reading here. In confrontation the typical abusive epithets indicate the polarity: the teachers of English call the teachers of Reading 'skilly', and the teachers of Reading hurl back in return the criticism 'woolly'! It is difficult to sense which is the worst abuse, but easy to realize that the polarities have been institutionalized. Thus, on the whole, the teacher of English expects the pupil to be able to read, which means his job is to teach *about* literature. Hence an emphasis on genre, authors' biographies, and literary history. Conversely, the teacher of Reading merely 'uses' literature. This was well illustrated at a large conference of the New England Reading Association, where after stand after stand of schemes, kits, spirit masters, and charts to help the pupil learn to read, one salesman was loudly declaiming the value of the 'supplementary material' which his firm offered. This supplementary material proved to be boxes of books!

The report considers the possibility of recommending separate reading specialists, 'Reading Consultants', and 'Reading Departments' (paras 8.6 and 8.7). Indeed it goes as far as to say that 'some aspects of this concentrated attention were impressive'. However, the Committee pulled back with horror at the implications of the specialism, pointing out that: 'the disadvantages out-weighed the benefits. Although there was no "horizontal split" in the teaching of reading, there was a very sharp "vertical" split between reading and English' (8.7). In refusing this split, the report refused all others, linking the imaginative with the practical, the personal with the technical, the literary with the factual, and, indeed, all kinds of reading, even discipline and class control: 'the subtle aims we have outlined in the Report cannot be achieved unless there is peace in the classrooms' (15.27).

This final characteristic of the Report, a unity of approach, is the central force behind the whole-school language policy, growing out of what the Report calls 'the organic relationship between the various aspects of English, and . . . the need for continuity in their development throughout school life' (Plan, p. XXXV). This unity of the report has four perspectives. It is a call for interrelationship:

1. between the modes of language: talk, writing, listening, and reading;
2. between the uses of language: imaginative and practical;
3. between the different learning activities across the curriculum;
4. through the ages of schooling.

Unfortunately we are a long way from this unity in professional work. Those who have studied reading in this country are considerably less interested in talk. Those who have devoted professional concern to problems of pupils' writing are often notably uninterested in problems of reading. Those who have specialized in literature are frequently badly read in linguistics. Indeed the bibliographies of key works for teachers in each of these fields barely overlap at all. Yet those of us working to help actual pupils term after term must produce a unity of all these aspects. The Report seems to me the first comprehensive and unified approach to language development.

Even post-Bullock there is a real risk of fragmentation within the language effort. In some schools the 'language policy' is mainly directed to 'correcting' writing, in others, seemingly more knowledgeable, talking and writing are the focus. Reading beyond the initial stages is given a high priority in some other, though fewer, schools. (This lower priority comes, I suspect, from the fact that much work on reading has been American.) It is rarer and difficult to find a truly integrated approach, just as it is rare to find a truly integrated approach from conference, speaker, or specialist writer. This is a pity, and surprising in view of the close integration of the report.

The task of school leadership, then, is to develop this unity within the school, so that all teachers can draw upon the insights and techniques of the various specialists.

3. Language and Education

Dr W. A. Gatherer

The nature of language

We do not know how language came into existence. For thousands of years, civilized man has pondered the nature of language, and from earliest times there have been theories as to its origins and characteristics. Modern scholars have tended to discount speculation about the historical origins of language, on the grounds that we simply do not have sufficient evidence to make useful hypotheses. While the development of particular languages is still studied by historical linguists, the main emphasis of modern linguistic scholarship lies in the study of language as it is observed in the actual world.

Attempts have been made to infer the origin of language from studies of speech-acquisition by infants. But children learn their mother tongue in an environment which is entirely different from that of primitive man; they acquire a language which is already established and in use; and in any case we are far from having a natural history of language acquisition to draw upon for data. Another way which has been attempted is to try to infer from so-called 'primitive' languages some of the features which may have characterized man's early language activity. But there are no primitive languages. However primitive may be the economies or cultures of aboriginals, their languages are fully developed. Their vocabularies and grammars are no less complex or systematic than the languages of the most highly civilized peoples. Another field of study which has been used to try to throw light on the origins of language is zoology. The communication systems of animals, however—even of apes, which are physiologically nearer to man—are so different from human language that there would seem to be no possibility of comparing them in any illuminating way. What we must do, modern scholars have concluded, is examine language as we find it, as it is used as an important aspect of human behaviour.

There have been hundreds of attempts to define language, and different schools of linguistic scholarship have approached it in different ways. Usually, however, you can look at language in either one of two ways: as a system of signs, or as a kind of social behaviour. These are equally valid viewpoints and your choice of approach will normally depend on your particular interest—that is, whether you are interested in the *analysis* of language or whether your main concern is with the *uses* of language. Modern scholars generally take the view that language is too complex a phenomenon to be defined in brief, and in any case the word *language* has undergone such a semantic spread or radiation of meaning as to preclude any really worthwhile definition. It is preferable to *describe* the characteristics of language. Thus we can work towards a description of the structure of language and then consider the functions of language.

When we think of language as a set of signs, we must be clear that the *signs* are distinguishable from *symbols*. A sign is a token, a mark or device with a special meaning attached to it—for example, animal noises, such as a cat's purring or a dog's bark, are signs of the animal's feelings. But they are not symbols, for symbols represent things because they are selected to do so. Symbols are conventional signs, like the shapes on maps which signify railways, churches, and golf courses. Language uses arbitrary symbols; that is, a word or a phrase cannot be thought of as a 'natural' or 'inevitable' embodiment of a meaning. Many people are unaware that words are wholly conventional signs which convey nothing of their meaning in their sound or shape. An illustration of this is the old joke about the Italian who invented a pasta and was asked why he called it *spaghetti*: he said 'Because it looks like spaghetti, it feels like spaghetti and it tastes like spaghetti'. Like Aldous Huxley's character who, looking at some pigs, said 'Rightly is they called *pigs*', people tend to confuse the linguistic symbol with the thing it symbolizes. A moment's thought, however, about the linguistic symbols used by different languages to represent the same thing will prove this point: the term *horse* in English denotes the same thing as is denoted by the very different words *hippos, equus, Pferd*, and *cheval*. Onomatopoetic words like *tick, cuckoo, dingdong* are partial exceptions to the rule, for they do to some extent imitate actual noises; but even with this type of word the arbitrariness of linguistic symbolism can be shown by the fact that different word-sounds are used for similar noises in different languages: for example a French cat goes *ron-ron*, not *purr-purr*; in German the sound of a bell is *Bim-Bam* and a door banging is represented by *knapps*.

The symbols of which language consists are primarily the sounds of speech. M. A. K. Halliday suggests that language can be thought of as *organized noise*, and most linguists agree that speech should be regarded as the primary substance of language. Speech comes first, in the history of man as a species and in the development of the individual. Some linguists point out that to speak of 'written language' is misleading, for writing is merely a record of language; but most modern scholars now regard writing as another form or mode of language. The sound substance or phonology of a language consists of a finite number of units which linguists call phonemes. A phoneme is a minimum significant sound used by a particular language—significant because the phoneme marks the difference between the meaning of a word as against any other word. For example, it is the initial phoneme which contrasts the meaning of *bin* and *pin, tin* and *chin*. The linguist recognizes the sounds /*b*/, /*p*/, /*t*/ and /*ch*/ as distinctive features; of course, the /*i*/ sound and the /*n*/ sound are also phonemes. Note that in the sound of the word *bib*, the initial /*b*/ is a different *sound* from the final /*b*/; but the linguist recognizes both instances as manifestations of the same phoneme. Because the initial phoneme is different in its actual sound from the end-phoneme, we class both sounds as *allophones* of the phoneme /*b*/. (The diagonal lines are used to 'mark off' a phoneme.) All languages use a range of between 20 and 50 phonemes, but different languages will, of course, use different sets of the phonemes available to the human voice. English uses about 46 phonemes: the precise number cannot be stated because it will depend on the dialect you speak. It will also depend on the way you define a phoneme, for linguists are by no means unanimous as to what a phoneme really is: the term has been called a 'logical fiction' because linguists do not agree as to its definition; but they do agree that it is a useful and meaningful term.

The phoneme is thus the 'atom' or smallest unit of language. But it has no distinctive meaning: that is, by itself, a phoneme cannot carry what we would normally recognize as a meaning. The smallest unit of language which bears meaning is the *morpheme*. Like the phoneme, the morpheme is not a universally agreed concept, but it is another very useful term in linguistic analysis. The morpheme is the smallest individually meaningful unit in an utterance. The word *uneatable*, for example, can be divided into the morphemes *un, eat* and *able*. Every word can be analysed into one or more morphemes. A *free* morpheme is one that can constitute a word by itself, and a *bound* morpheme is one which never occurs alone, being always found along with at least one other morpheme. In the word *uneatable*, for example, *un-* is a bound morpheme. In this particular word, *-able* is actually a bound morpheme, though it may appear at first sight to be a free morpheme: but it is not the same morpheme as the free form *able* in such an utterance as *He's able*. Morphemes can also be divided into *roots* and *affixes*, an affix being a bound morpheme used to extend or modify the meaning of a word, and a root being a bound or free morpheme which remains when all affixes have been removed. For example, in *uneatable*, *un-* and *-able* are affixes, and *eat* is the root. Every word 'contains' a root, many words consisting of a single root.

The word *word* has been used frequently in preceding paragraphs without definition. It is, in fact, difficult to define a word. Aristotle defined the word as 'the smallest significant unit of speech'. But linguists have reserved that role for the morpheme. And what does 'significant' mean? Does *to* have a meaning in itself? Leonard Bloomfield, the father of 'structural' linguistics, gives the classic definition of a word as a *minimum free form*, that is a unit which can have meaning when used alone. But as Otto Jespersen, the great Danish grammarian, points out, there are many forms which are not free but which are given the status of word (for example, the French *je* or the Russian *K* [towards]) and others which normally do not occur as free forms, such as the English *the* and *a*. Bloomfield also suggests that a word can be characterized as a form which cannot be 'interrupted' by another form. For instance a phrase such as *Look here* can be interrupted by the insertion of a preposition—*Look over here*, *Look under here*. But *Look* cannot have another form intelligibly inserted in it—you cannot say *L-over-ook* or *o-look-ver* or *l-here-ook* or *he-over-re*. (It is true that in certain English styles you can jokingly embed one form in another— for example, *Abso-blooming-lutely!*—but this is an abnormal occurrence.)

The academic difficulty in defining a word emerges from linguists' preoccupation with language as speech and their insistent search for 'linguistic universals', that is characteristic features of all languages. In spoken utterance we do not normally separate off 'words' except perhaps when speaking very slowly as when dictating—and even then we may separate off forms which we would not accept as words: for example: *I'm go-ing to Jugo-slavia*. At the same time, we have all been trained to space out the forms we call words when we write. The recognition of the word as a unit is a universally held ability in users of human language. The very fact that we normally think of a word as the unit we separate off by white spaces on the page indicates that we have an intuitional awareness of 'wordness', even though we can recognize that it is difficult to be precise about what *word* means. To think of a word as *the smallest unit of language which can stand alone and still have meaning in itself* is good enough for all practical purposes.

Morphology, the relationships of morphemes, has been called 'the grammar within words'.[1] The combining of words into larger structures is syntax. Both morphology and syntax are included in the domain of grammar. Before we consider grammar, however, it will be worthwhile to discuss the relationship between grammar and *lexis*, the vocabulary of a language.

Lexicology is the study of words and their relationships with one another, where these relationships are outside grammar. Thus the associative habits of a word—their likelihood of appearing in a sequence along with other words—is called *collocation*. A *lexical set* is a set of words that generally collocate with one another: for example, *wine*, *water*, *beer* and *milk* form a lexical set which will usually collocate with such words as *bottle*, *drink*, *spill* and so on. The *thesaurus* of a language is a collection of words in lexical sets; thus the thesaurus tells us a number of words that can usually be substituted for a given word without excessive loss of meaning. The dictionary of a language is a list of the words used by the language, the number of words included being limited by the lexicographer's editorial strategy (the size or price etc.) and the state of his current knowledge.

[1] H. A. L. Gleason, Jr, *Linguistics and English Grammar*, Holt, Rinehart & Winston, 1965, p. 164.

Some words form a closed system: there is a finite and identifiable number of them used in a language. Examples in English are the prepositions, the articles *a, an, the,* and the pronouns. Most words, however, are members of an *open set*: there can be no end to the number of words which can be substituted for them in a grammatical utterance. For example, in the sentence frame

$$/// \text{The}// \qquad\qquad // \text{is}// \qquad\qquad ///$$

the blank spaces can be filled by an infinite number of possibilities. (Even if one could exhaust all the known words ever invented, one could carry on inventing words which grammatically fit the space.)

Returning to Halliday's suggestion that language can be thought of as 'organized noise', we can see how the phonemic and morphemic organization of vocal sound gives language form. For a complete description of language we must account for the *substance*—that is, the sound and the writing—and the *form*. Also, as will be seen, we must describe the ways in which linguistic forms are used in human intercourse. The study of linguistic sound substance is phonology.

LINGUISTIC SCIENCES				
Phonetics - - - - - - - - - -				
	Linguistics - - - - - - - - - - - - - - - -			
SUBSTANCE		FORM		SITUATION (environment)
phonic	phonology	grammar lexis	context	extra-textual features

I

The study of linguistic form involves examining the grammar and the vocabulary of languages—how the units of form are related together in words and sentences. What language means in human situations is the concern of semantic studies. Thus the form we impose upon the substance of language is seen to consist of grammar and lexis.

Before we discuss the nature of grammar it is important to consider the different schools of thought which have contributed to our knowledge of language in modern times. The so-called Prague School has influenced our thinking on the relationship between the structure of

[1] M. A. K. Halliday, in *Patterns of Language*, Longman, 1966.

language and the uses to which it is put in social intercourse. Their interest in the functional aspects of language has been paralleled to some extent by the British School, of which Firth is the acknowledged founder. Firth's interest in 'the context of situation' and the ways in which language interacts with social and cultural influences inspired much of the most important linguistic scholarship of our time. In America there have been two extremely influential schools, the 'structuralists' or Bloomfieldians and the 'transformationalists' or Chomskyans.

Structuralism may be said to be a preoccupation with the classification of the elements of language. Structural linguistics as a discipline owes most to the work of Leonard Bloomfield (1887–1949) whose book, *Language* (1933) established the notion that linguistic scholarship should confine its attention to the 'observable facts' of language as it is spoken, its aim being to classify the 'corpus' of linguistic data at different levels: first the phonemes, then the morphemes, then the words and word classes, then the sentences and sentence-types. Bloomfield argued that this was a rigorous scientific process, and that it should exclude aspects of language which could not be treated with precision and objectivity, such as the analysis of meaning or the intuitions of the native speaker. The discovery procedures employed by structuralist linguists were used with great effect in their descriptions of American Indian languages, and they have thrown much light on the nature of the phonological, morphological, and syntactical process by which language operates.

Noam Chomsky's first book, *Syntactic Structures* (1957), and the many works by him and his followers published since then, represent an entirely different view of the purposes of linguistics. Chomsky's training was in structural linguistics, but he found that the methods which had worked so effectively in the analysis of phonemic and morphemic forms did not satisfactorily apply to sentences. The lists of phonemes and morphemes in a given language are finite (though a list of morphemes would be very long) but it is impossible to list the sentences of any natural language. There can be no limit to the number of sentences that can be produced by a speaker of any language. It is infinite. Language therefore has a 'generative' or 'creative' or 'open-ended' character which cannot be accounted for by the methodology of structuralist linguistics. A language consists of an indefinitely large corpus of utterances, and no grammatical description of language can be adequate unless it accounts for the grammar's capability of generating sentences. An acceptable grammar must be seen as a 'device' of some sort (the term *device* is an abstraction, having nothing to do with physical or mechanical processes) for producing the sentences of a language. Further, the grammar must be capable of generating all the *grammatical* sentences of a language and none of the *ungrammatical* ones which speakers can produce on occasions owing to slips of memory or some psychophysical defect. Chomsky's work, and that of the Chomskyan school generally, has been largely devoted to difficult and often abstruse attempts to produce a 'scientific' grammar of English that satisfies these conditions. Chomsky's influence on linguistic scholarship has been deep and pervasive. Every linguistic scholar of note who has published work in the last decade has had to take Chomskyan ideas into account. The most important non-Chomskyan grammatical models, such as Halliday's 'scale and category' grammar and Sydney Lamb's 'stratificational' grammar, are *generative* in the sense that they attempt to fulfil the same objectives as Chomsky prescribed for grammars, even though they employ quite different procedures and conceptual frameworks.

When we think of language as a kind of social behaviour, we must look to the disciplines of anthropology and sociology in combination with general linguistics. Edward Sapir (1884–1939) reminds us that 'language is a cultural or social product, and must be understood as such'.[1] Anthropological linguistics has thrown much light on the nature of language, particularly by demonstrating that language is a means of categorizing and ordering human experience. The linguistic habits of people who are members of a particular society contribute to the formation of a 'world-view' which is to some extent peculiar to themselves. As Benjamin Lee Whorf put it: 'We dissect nature along lines laid down by our native languages'.[2] According to this school of thought, the way we think about or perceive our environment is deeply affected (not to say distorted) by the language we have acquired as native speakers. But the 'Whorfian hypothesis' cannot be accepted unreservedly: it is difficult for members of very different cultures to form reliable insights to one another's ways of thinking, and the kinds of relations between language and thought upon which the theory rests are by no means well established. At the same time, studies of the role of language habits in the enculturation of the young in different societies continue to illuminate our linguistic knowledge. It seems unquestionable that there are close perceptible relationships between the way we learn to speak and the way we learn to think. Just as we use language to rationalize our environment, so the environment in which we live influences our language and language habits.

The association of linguistics and sociology has become extremely close and important in recent years. Sociolinguistics may be said to be the study of language as a 'mode of action', to use a phrase of the great anthropologist, Malinowski; but although there has been a great deal of recent work in this field scholars are reluctant to claim it as a specific discipline. Halliday has said that he has been 'doing socio-

---

[1] E. Sapir, in *Culture, Language and Personality*, D. G. Mandelbaum (ed.), University of California Press, 1961.

[2] B. L. Whorf, in *The Psychology of Language, Thought and Instruction*, J. P. De Cecco (ed.), Holt, Rinehart & Winston, 1969.

linguistics' all his life but has always called it linguistics.[1] All the great linguists have been concerned with the relationship between language and social interaction. The social functions of language, how it transmits cultural ideas and attitudes, how it relates to the social structure, how it helps or hinders the socialization of the young, are all current preoccupations of linguists, and their studies have contributed valuably to our understanding of language and how it works.

To sum up our present position in man's ceaseless effort to describe the nature of language, a few generalizations may be found useful. Some of these represent accounts that have been made briefly in preceding pages, and others will indicate topics which will be dealt with in following sections.

1. *Language is primarily speech.* All the written language that ever existed is but the froth on an ocean of speech. Man is *homo loquens*, and it is speech that makes him human.

2. *Language is systemic.* However confusing and amorphous language may appear as we contemplate it as a human activity, language can be described systematically and scientifically. Rules can be discerned which govern its patterning and its cohesion.

3. *Language is dynamic.* It is constantly changing, never static. Its rules are never rigid and immutable.

4. *Language is social.* Every speaker speaks as a member of a particular community, and his language is partially a result of its traditions, values and social attitudes. Language cannot be wholly understood except in relation to the other human institutions with which it interacts.

5. *Language is personal.* Every speaker directs, modifies and regulates every act of speech according to the personal intentions with which he utters, according also to the purposes that lie behind his utterance, and according also to the state of emotions in which he happens to be when he makes an utterance.

6. *Language is meaningful.* Language expresses thought, and arouses thought in others. The symbolism of language enables both speaker and hearer to discern meaning, often of a different kind from that intended.

Acquisition and development

The relationship of language and thought has occupied the minds of scholars for centuries, and the growth of psychology and linguistics

[1] M. A. K. Halliday, in *Problems of Language and Learning*, A. Davies (ed.), Heinemann Educational, 1975.

has produced a massive literature on the subject. For the educational-
ist it is important to examine the various theories and conceptual
frameworks adduced to explain the manner in which children develop
their linguistic competence, since our teaching strategies will rely on
the theoretical validity and practical effectiveness of our conceptions
of language acquisition and development. An understanding of how
children learn should underlie our decisions about how we should
teach them. The most influential learning theories in the modern
educational scene are those propounded by the behaviourist psychologists and those of the Piagetian or developmental psychologists.
Chomskyan linguists have contributed certain notions about the
nature of language learning which must also be taken into account;
and the work of J. S. Bruner and his associates must also be given
attention.

Behaviourists develop their theory of language learning from their
observation of the visible behaviour of animals and children. The
fullest account of this learning theory was given by B. F. Skinner in
his book *Verbal Behaviour* (1957), but the theory has been developed
and explicated since then by many psychologists and psycholinguists.
The theory has been labelled S-R (Stimulus-Response) because it
stipulates that effective behaviour consists of producing satisfactory
responses to satisfactory stimuli. It states, to put it simply, that if a
child produces a linguistic response which the mother or other care-
taker accepts as appropriate he will be rewarded with some indicator
of approval. Consequently the child will tend to produce the same
response to the same stimulus in similar circumstances. The response
is reinforced by the reward. If the response is not satisfactory the
mother will not reinforce it and it will tend not to recur. This account
can be held to explain how it is that a child produces speech and also
how he learns to understand speech. It does not, however, tell us
anything about how the child's utterances (responses) came to be
made; this is accounted for by learning theorists in terms of imitation:
the mother's behaviour is a secondary means of reinforcement because
the child finds it satisfying to imitate her. According to Skinner, the
mother will reinforce responses which at first only approximate to
the desired response, and by a series of such reinforcements gradually
'shapes' the child's behaviour towards the behaviour she recognizes
to be 'correct' or 'appropriate'.

The Russian psychologist, I. P. Pavlov, argued that a response to
one stimulus can be elicited by another, associated, stimulus. Pavlov's
classic example of the dog's salivating in response to the ringing of
a bell in place of the sight of food is still the best illustration of this
'contiguity theory'. Learning theorists have adapted this notion to
language acquisition: thus we have the theory of mediation, which
states that a word can operate as a mediating stimulus, producing
a response in the absence of the original physical stimulus. Thus
through the mediation of language all kinds of associations can be

built between objects. Children learn what words mean by associating the meanings of known words with new words they are used alongside: for example, if a child is told that a library is a house for holding books he will connect *house* and *holding* and *books* to form an idea of the meaning of library. Mediation theory can also account for the way a child acquires the ability to produce sentences he has never heard before. The explanation is that different sets of words are classified grammatically in the child's mind by occurring in the same place in the framework of an utterance: thus by hearing the strings 'See the book', 'See the man', 'See the train', and so on the child learns to produce a new utterance by inserting a known word in the place previously occupied by other known words.

It has become fashionable to reject learning theory outright because it fails to account adequately for various known facts about language development. But it must be conceded that learning theorists are still actively investigating language activity, and our knowledge is continuously being increased. It would be wrong to dismiss the theory on the grounds that its explanatory power is weak, since further and more refined explanations are still being produced. Moreover the theory should not be rejected on the grounds that it is mechanistic and takes no account of the innate capacity for learning that some psychologists have shown children to possess, for behaviourist theories do not preclude the existence of innateness of various kinds. Educationists must not ignore learning theory, for it has given us valuable insights and suggested teaching strategies of great importance, for example in the teaching of basal reading and number.

The most notable critic of behaviourist learning theory is Chomsky, who approaches language acquisition in an entirely different way. Chomsky argues that a child must be born with some kind of knowledge of language programmed into his brain. Without this postulate of a 'Language Acquisition Device' it is impossible to account for children's ability to achieve linguistic competence. The linguistic 'input' the child gets from adults is necessarily limited and deficient, fragmented and full of irregularities. The child cannot learn the language from the utterances he hears unless he possesses some innate 'universal grammar' which enables him to perceive the 'grammaticality' or acceptability of a sentence and to utter grammatically correct sentences which he has never heard before. Chomsky supports this argument by pointing out that children learn to speak at an early age, before the development of general cognitive faculties: that their ability to acquire their mother tongue has little to do with general intelligence (after all, stupid children learn to speak)—or motivation (lazy children learn to speak): and that formal language teaching is unnecessary for the acquisition process.

The *faculté de langage* postulated by Chomsky has no demonstrable psychological reality, but it is a powerful concept, particularly in its general relationship with pedagogical theory. Although Chomsky's theories have no direct application to teaching, since they involve highly technical linguistic and philosophical hypotheses, they have affected many educationalists' attitudes to language learning. W. B. Currie has stated the case: 'Native speakers seem to show at the initial stage of language learning that they have underlying faculties which make learning possible. This also makes language learning personal and . . . "creative".' Currie suggests that the 'universal ideas of language' which lie behind learning processes are best thought of as 'underlying semantic notions from which the child organizes the deep dependencies and relationships of his language'.[1] He argues that the most effective teaching relies upon 'inductive methods' which ally the child's intuitions and 'native experience' with material—speech of writing in the case of language work—which offers him opportunities for hypothetizing and discussing and ultimately 'discovering' for himself the principle to be learned.

Chomsky insists on the existence of a genetically inherited capacity which is specifically linguistic. Many psychologists, on the other hand, base their view of language learning on Piaget's theory of innate cognitive mechanisms. Piaget sees learning as resulting from the intellectual processes of assimilation and accommodation, both of which are functions of the organism's need for adaptation. The child is born with certain *schemes* and *schemata* or behaviour patterns which act on environmental stimuli: for example, because he instinctively sucks the nipple he will suck someone's finger using the same scheme of actions. This is the process of assimilation. As a result of interaction with a new feature of the environment the schemata are changed to cope with the new situation: for example, the assimilatory behaviour involved in picking up something within reach will be changed when he crawls along the floor to pick the object up. This is the process of accommodation. More and more complex schemata are developed as the child matures. The child's development proceeds through a continuous process of generalizations and differentiations, each phase involving a repetition of the previous processes but moving towards a higher level of organization. The developmental continuum can be divided into three major phases: the sensori-motor phase (age 0 to 2); the phase during which there is a preparation for conceptual thought (roughly ages 2 to 11); and the phase of cognitive thinking (ages 11 to 12 upwards).

Applied to language acquisition, Piaget's theory of cognitive development provides powerful new insights. When new stimuli are presented, the child's reaction is governed by the structures he can currently command. He interprets and applies new linguistic information in terms of what he already knows. He assimilates and accommodates language substance as he encounters it. Piaget himself has not been directly concerned with language development, and research by psycholinguists using the Piagetian conceptual framework is still

[1] W. B. Currie, *New Directions in Teaching English Language*, Longman, 1973.

at an early stage. Nevertheless a valuable conception of language development is emerging—that it proceeds through the interaction of active experimentation by the child and the internalized cognitive structures he possesses at a given stage.

The Russian school of psycholinguistic studies, founded by Vygotsky in the 1920s and extensively publicized by Luria, regards language as an essential factor in mental growth. Vygotsky and Luria do not accept the Piagetian notion of inevitable development: it is the interaction of language and situation in a social context, the Russians believe, which gives the child the capacity to organize his mental activities. Language therefore plays a crucial role in mental development. Since rational, intentional communication between minds is impossible without speech, says Vygotsky, the growth of a child's thinking ability and the growth of his linguistic competence are concomitant with and closely related to his social development. The internalization of speech, at about the age of seven, leads to the development of higher forms of intellectual capability. Interaction with adults encourages mental development.

The work of Jerome S. Bruner has also been of great importance in developing our understanding of the relationship of language and mental development. As an educational psychologist, Bruner holds that mental development passes through three main stages of readiness, the enactive, the iconic, and the symbolic. These stages, reminiscent of Piaget's stages of pre-operational, concrete-operational and formal-operational, are accompanied by appropriate stages of mental need. In his eloquent and influential expositions of the nature of 'discovery learning', Bruner argues that learning depends on the opportunities provided to allow the pupil to explore his environment in terms of his own needs and capacities: 'Discovery teaching generally involves not so much the process of leading students to discover what is "out there", but, rather, their discovering what is in their own heads.'[1] Teachers must let pupils use what they know. Bruner uses the notion of *compatibility* (which appears to contain echoes of Piaget's notions of assimilation and accommodation): new knowledge will only be truly possessed by a child when it has been connected with his existing repertoire of ideas and knowledge.[2] He urges educators to appreciate the need to give pupils training in such processes as 'pushing an idea to its limits'—for 'going beyond the information given' is the most important characteristic of man as a thinker. He argues the need to encourage a pupil to reflect upon and evaluate his or her own thinking processes. Language, Bruner points out, makes this 'self-loop' easier, as when the child realizes that the same concept can be expressed by completely different words.

Bruner believes that the 'channelling capacity' (the ability to

[1] J. S. Bruner, 'Some elements of discovery', in *Learning by Discovery: A Critical Approach*, L. S. Shulman and G. R. Keislar, Rand McNally, 1966.
[2] This idea is echoed by the Bullock Report, 4.9.

handle information) can be improved when information is organized in suitable ways appropriate to particular situations. The main advantage of discovery learning is that it increases the pupil's intellectual potency: he develops the ability to devise strategies of approach and effective learning structures. The way in which he structures his learning in a given lesson will help his understanding of regularities and relationships at other times. Bruner conceives this structuring process as an ability to 'code' information. Language enables us to codify the input of our senses, and thus to organize and make sense of our experience. The coding ability of the human mind allows us to create and to comprehend meaningful language out of all the raw linguistic substance available to us.

In a recently published paper[1] Bruner outlines some of his recent thinking on language and cognition. He proposes the term 'species minimum' to connote the basic linguistic competence postulated by Chomsky and others who claim the existence of innate language capability possessed by all speakers of all natural languages. Beyond this linguistic competence there is another kind called 'communicative competence' which includes the ability to make and understand utterances in accordance with the circumstances in which they are made. Bruner suggests that this kind of competence is also 'species minimum' in the sense that every normal person can be expected to achieve it without special training. Communicative competence, says Bruner, can be taken to involve the achievement of the 'concrete operations' described by Piagetian psychologists. Beyond this innate, species-minimum competence, however, there is what Bruner calls 'analytic competence' which, as with Piaget's 'formal operations', involves 'the prolonged operation of thought processes exclusively on linguistic representations, on propositional structures, accompanied by strategies of thought and problem-solving appropriate not to direct experience with objects and events but with ensembles of propositions.'

In this view, language is seen as an instrument of thought. If we set aside the highly technical arguments adduced by Bruner to explicate his conception of the psychological relationships between language and cognition, we may regard his postulate of analytic competence as the ability to use language *for* thinking. Analytic competence is not acquired 'naturally', as is communicative competence, but is acquired through formal education by means of being engaged in intellectual pursuits. In school, knowledge is 'decontextualized', made abstract, and schooling demands analytic competence for the pursuits it requires of the students.[2]

[1] J. S. Bruner, 'Language as an Instrument of Thought', in A. Davies (ed.), *Problems of Language and Learning*, Heinemann Educational Books, 1975.

[2] This latter elaboration of the theory is based on a revised paper by Bruner and Karen L. Peterson which is summarized by Alan Davies, *op. cit.*

That the mental skills involved in the higher-order uses of language are not acquired without the intervention of the educator is a fundamental assumption in modern research and development. Much effort is being expended on attempts to identify these higher-order skills, and at every stage in the educational process there are strategies now being proposed to facilitate their development. The nursery school curriculum is being profoundly influenced by the work of Dr Joan Tough and her associates in the Schools Council project, 'Communication Skills in Early Childhood'. Tough takes the view that the most productive activity in early childhood education is the child–adult dialogue, carefully devised by a trained adult to give the child experience of 'thinking strategies' which will become internalized through practice. She has described a range of such strategies and her project is concerned with developing teachers' awareness of the skills of thinking and language-use that children can achieve and giving teachers training in the use of dialogue to promote the growth of these skills.[1]

For older primary pupils similar programmes relating language-use and thinking are being produced: *Concept 7–9*, for example, provides children with problems which have to be discussed in group work, so that they explore their own linguistic resources, and share those of others, to find the means to arrive at practical solutions and decisions. For an older age-group, such programmes as *Man A Course of Study* provide pupils with the techniques of acquiring data about their environment and lead them into 'thinking strategies' which are their own rather than externally imposed routines. The Schools Council project, 'Writing Across the Curriculum', carries the study of the relationship between language and thinking into the secondary school stage, and is producing some interesting studies of the learning process at work in the classroom.

In their descriptions of the processes of thinking, psychologists have accorded an important role to concept formation. The young child forms concepts of objects, sounds and feelings which are internalized representations of categories of experience. With the acquisition of language many of these concepts are verbally labelled and recognized. Concepts may be acquired easily by means of hearing or reading verbal formulations of their content, but some are so complex that they cannot be grasped without a preliminary sequence of 'leading up' concepts or a series of experiences which offer instances (and noninstances) of the concept. In school, the two most common methods of presenting concepts to pupils are to offer verbal formulations and to offer 'practical' experiences which exemplify the concepts. Almost all teaching is a process of presenting concepts in these ways.

The role of verbal formulation is obviously of great importance in the teaching of all subjects in the secondary school. Much of the

[1] Bullock Report, 5–8, and forthcoming papers.

teacher's skill in communicating concepts relies on the language he chooses to convey his meanings. Similarly, much of the pupil's success in understanding what is being taught lies in his ability to transmute the teacher's language into concepts. Most teachers know that the copious presentation of examples facilitates understanding; but many appear to show less appreciation of the role of the language used. Barnes and others have pointed out that many teachers tend in expounding their subject to use language which some pupils fail to understand.[1] If the pupil's access to technical terms is limited he will not acquire the prerequisite concepts which lead to understanding.

Specialist teachers may use a specialist language containing forms with which the pupil is not acquainted, or of which he is only vaguely aware; and even when the teacher is very well aware of the important role played by language he may simply not know how best to communicate, in effective linguistic interchange, the concepts whose verbal formulations are so familiar to himself. Such concepts in mathematics as *oppositeness* and *magnitude* may be quite difficult for a child to attain without extensive experience of instances, but may be very difficult for the teacher to exemplify in a short space of time. Teachers of history may freely use such terms as *state* and *government* without being fully aware of the inchoateness of the pupils' understanding of the concepts. There is, moreover, a 'language of secondary education', which, apart from technical terminology, may constitute a barrier to comprehension. This is the 'textbook' style of discourse teachers tend to use in their exposition of a subject. The complexity of the sentence structure, the unfamiliarity of the vocabulary, the abstractness of the concepts may all obscure the meaning for the pupils.

For the educator, then, the most important thing about language is that it is essential for thinking. Although we do not know what the precise relationship between language and thinking is, it is evident that language enables us to communicate our thought. If some form of thinking is possible without language, it is nevertheless language which gives our thinking form, sequence and coherence, and it is by means of language that we give substance to our thought. We may think of language as a *clothing* of thought, but it is more satisfactory to think of it as the embodiment of thought in the way that a melody is the embodiment of the sounds of music. Thus we think *in* language; and effective thinking is not possible unless we possess linguistic competencies adequate enough to realize and express our ideas.

The pupil who, being told to 'Think before you speak' says, 'How do I know what I think till I hear what I say?' is expressing an important idea for teachers. 'Speaking one's thoughts' is in a real sense the very act of thinking. It is in the verbal teasing out of one's thinking that one learns to think effectively. Speech is therefore the primary instrument of thought and there is a process of 'talking one's way

[1] D. Barnes, 'Language in the Secondary Classroom', in *Language, the Learner and the School*, Penguin, 1971.

through' ideas which is essential to learning. Teachers of all subjects should be sensitively aware of the potentiality of this process. Pupils will not learn the thinking process of an academic discipline merely by listening or taking notes. They must *engage* in the language of the subject if they are to grasp its concepts. Learning physics is as much a process of learning to *talk physics* as anything else; and the teacher who merely insists on silence—or who fails to incite talk about his subject—fails to perceive the necessary connection between speech, thought and learning.

It is not enough, moreover, to expect pupils to engage in formal academic talk in the process of learning. Speech is a social activity and the speech which induces learning must not be divorced from the social situation in which it occurs. Pupils should freely express their thoughts, feelings and needs in the process of teacher–pupil inter-action, so that they, the learners, can control their own learning. It is curious that many teachers who recognize the value of the 'Ah-hah! experience' in learning would greet spontaneously uttered 'Ah-hahs!' with disapproval, yet this kind of verbal recognition of understanding is a natural aid to learning, even in the privacy of the study. More importantly, learning requires the verbal marks of questioning. In every classroom pupils should be free to express their lack of compre-hension, or to express their guesses or tentative formulations of a solution to a problem. Again, learning is a two-way process: when a pupil feels that the teacher should repeat or rephrase a statement he should be free to regulate the teacher's behaviour to accommodate his own thought processes; yet most teachers would object to being told to do this by a pupil.

Where a teacher is engaged in conveying the content and discipline of an academic subject, then, the process should involve the functional use of speech in various ways. Teacher and pupils should be caught up in a continuous dialogue in which ideas are assimilated by means of talk and listening, questioning and answering, *on the pupils' part* and on the pupils' initiative so far as this is consonant with the requirements of the classroom. A one-to-one tutorial, in which the student plays an active role, is often the ideal learning situation; but schools can seldom provide it. To obtain the benefits of closely per-sonalized learning within the limitations of the institutionalized classroom is one of the principal objectives of good teaching.

Wittgenstein pointed out that one can think with a pen in one's hand as well as in one's head. The verbal teasing out of one's thought which is characterized by 'thinking aloud' can also be achieved by means of expressive writing: that is, by writing for oneself, for one's own benefit. This would seem to be a little-used pedagogical tech-nique outside the English classroom. Most teachers expect their pupils to have acquired the skills of written communication independ-ently and seem to consider that it is only the English teacher who need feel responsible for the teaching of composition. But writing is language, and though it has its own conventions and patterns it is dependent, for its efficacy as communication, on the same cognitive–linguistic skills as speech. To be able to write well on scientific or historical or technical matters it is necessary to be able to *think* well in the language of the subject. Expressive writing should therefore become a normal practice within the subject; for this promotes good thinking in the subject.

The ultimate sign of understanding a subject is the ability to convey one's knowledge in effective representational or transactional language. Most teachers expect a well-formed piece of exposition as an indication that something has been learned. Yet this is the most sophisticated of the language skills most of us acquire in life. It is not a part of learning to be able thus to convey information and ideas—rather it is the end-product of learning. It is unrealistic in teachers to look for this skill as if it were a natural acquisition, or something acquired somewhere other than in their own classrooms. Every teacher should attempt to teach the language skills essential to his or her own subjects.

Every teacher, furthermore, should be trained to be sensitive to the role of language in learning. This requires that every teacher should have a comprehensive knowledge of the nature of language, language-acquisition, and language learning. Successful teaching requires an awareness by the teacher of the linguistic processes involved in concept attainment and the reinforcement of what is comprehended. The teacher of history or science, as the Bullock Report puts it, must 'understand the process by which his pupils take possession of the historical or scientific information that is offered them'.

Language in the social context

Most natural languages exhibit degrees of variation in the patterns of lexical, grammatical and phonological choices which are habitually made by native speakers. One form of variation which assumes importance to the educator is *dialect*, which may be crudely defined as the form of a language identified as being peculiar to a particular geographical area or distinct community. A widely established language, such as English, German or French, will consist of a number of dialects, the 'language' itself being indefinable except as a set of dialects. The study of dialects (dialectology) has preoccupied amateur scholars for centuries; the identification of a dialect, however, is a highly technical process and the status of a dialect can only be established by painstaking and comprehensive descriptions of the differences in vocabulary, grammar and pronunciation between one linguistic community and all the others comprising the major language community.

In many languages, there are also 'cultural' linguistic variations discernible, so that the existence of social or subcultural dialects can be claimed. In English, French and other major languages a special status can be claimed for the language used commonly by educated people: thus 'standard English' may be regarded as a prestigious dialect of English, which carries the importance of mandarin Chinese as a universally accepted form of language. With respect to the grammar, Standard English (SE) is largely uniform among educated speakers all over the world (though there are minor differences). The same applies to the vocabulary, though again there are many words in common use in, say, the USA which are not familiar to speakers of SE in other parts of the English-speaking world. With respect to pronunciation, and particularly to accent, there are considerable variations, so that the nationality of different native English speakers can easily be heard: but these national differences are seldom great enough to prevent easy communication. The phonological variety of SE which has been used by British linguists to represent the standard is that of London and the English 'Public Schools'. Known as RP (Received Pronunciation) this variety of speech is used technically to provide norms for the purpose of making phonetic analyses of English speech. But RP must not be confused with SE: it does not represent the phonology of SE in any other part of the English-speaking world. It may be that there is a Welsh or Australian or Californian equivalent of RP.

Understandably the grammar of SE has come to be regarded as the 'correct' forms, and deviations appearing in subcultural 'non-standard' dialects are widely considered to be incorrect. To say *I seen him* is incorrect, is equivalent to saying that the SE speaker would not use that form, preferring *I saw him*. But *I seen him, I haven't done nothing*, and many other non-standard forms are characteristics of certain dialects whose lineage is at least as ancient as that of SE, and linguists are naturally averse to making value judgements which do not concern them as scientists. The structural linguists of the Bloomfieldian school were particularly insistent that their approach to language was objective and that consequently they could not regard any one form of language as intrinsically inferior or superior to any other form. Further, it has been cogently argued by Labov and others that non-standard English dialects are not radically different systems but are in fact closely related to SE.[1]

This objectivity, however, has led many writers to assert that it is improper to apply prescriptions of any kind to language use. Robert A. Hall Jr's book, *Leave Your Language Alone*, is a good example of this extreme attitude. Some of Hall's assertions, which he calls

[1] W. Labov, *The Study of Nonstandard English*, NCTE, 1969.

'basic principles', have become familiar shibboleths in educational discussion:

> There is no such thing as good and bad (or correct and incorrect, grammatical and ungrammatical, right and wrong) in language.
> All languages and dialects are of equal merit, each in its own way.
> 'Correct' can only mean 'socially acceptable' and apart from this has no meaning as applied to language.[1]

This attitude results from a confusion between the scientific aim of objectivity which is proper for the linguist to sustain in his studies and the educational aim of intervention with children's language for the purpose of increasing its range and power. Hall's assertions are also representative of the imprecision of language which causes so much confusion in teachers' minds when confronted with statements that naturally seem to contradict their own common sense.

As it reads, the statement that 'there is no such thing as correct and incorrect, grammatical and ungrammatical etc.' is manifestly nonsense: no linguist would hesitate to say that *The balls boys the kicks* is ungrammatical and therefore incorrect. What Hall really means, of course, is that the linguist is not concerned with telling people how they *ought* to speak but is equally interested in studying all language, whether it is socially acceptable or not. The educator cannot afford to take this lofty stance. To teachers, all languages and dialects are *not* of equal merit, since for various reasons they are obliged to aim at making the standard forms accessible to their pupils. It is true that *correctness* is usually equated with social acceptability in the popular mind: this is the case with all forms of behaviour, and it is not surprising (nor is it in any real sense pernicious) that it should be so with language. Using language is a rule-governed activity at various levels. Just as we learn the 'rules of use' in social situations, we have to learn the 'rules of effectiveness' in communication if we are to achieve any degree of mastery. It is just as foolish to abjure all notions of correctness as it is to adopt intolerant and snobbish attitudes towards any deviation from the subjectively established standard of propriety which exists only in the mind of the individual.

It is true that many people do adopt invalid notions of correctness with regard to dialectal usage. The tendency is to conflate deviations in grammar and lexis and pronunciation and to condemn the whole 'speech package' of a dialect speaker as being socially inferior and therefore 'incorrect'. It is important for the educator to be able to distinguish between deviations which are functional for learning and those which are merely matters of social prestige. Variations in accent are seldom of any educational significance: teachers who criticize the use of 'glottal stops' in Cockney speech, for example, are clearly unaware that this is a speech characteristic, in different forms, of *all* speakers of English. Variations in pronunciation *can* be

[1] Revised as *Linguistics and Your Language*, Doubleday, 1960.

of marginal importance: the Scots pupil must learn to use the SSE (Standard Scots English) pronunciation of such words as *mouse*, *rough*, *floor* if he wishes to be understood beyond the borders of his own community. Variations in lexis can be educationally significant in a different way: knowing and enjoying the differences can be a real aid to linguistic maturity. Variations in grammar tend to be educationally significant only in the later stages of schooling, when it becomes important for pupils to master the subtler rules of rhetoric and style.

Linguists are at pains to point out that there is nothing intrinsically (linguistically) inferior about dialectal forms. In grammar, especially, there can be no appeal to the superior logicality or consistence of standard forms. The use of double or multiple negatives, for example, is quite common in many languages and was widely used in Shakespeare's time; this habit still survives among 'élite' speakers in such idioms as *I shouldn't wonder if it didn't rain* which is not grammatically different from *I didn't never hit nobody*. Again, the use of a plural form of *you* (*youse*) in some dialects is manifestly more consistent than the SE usage since SE uses plural forms for all the other personal pronouns.

It is, of course, quite proper to call these dialect forms 'wrong' when they are used within the norms of SE: when we speak SE we ought to conform with its established grammar, lexis and phonology. By the same token, it would be 'wrong' to use SE forms when speaking any other dialect where there are forms in the dialect which are 'proper' to that dialect. In dramatic dialogue, for example, the playwright uses his 'ear' for language to produce the forms which conform to and so mark the dialect of each speaker. And dialect speakers are just as sensitive as SE speakers to the required conventions of their own speechways: indeed they may be able to switch from one speech package to another. (Very few bidialectals, however, have equally good command of both the dialects they speak.)

The role of language in educational underachievement has been much debated in recent years, and indeed our interest in this subject has generated much valuable research into language development. The most notable theorist in this field is Basil Bernstein, whose work in studying the relationship between social structure and language-use has had a world-wide influence on educational thinking. In an early paper Bernstein distinguished between what he called 'public' language and 'formal' language, public language being characterized by restricted syntax and 'implicit' meanings, formal language being characterized by more explicit meanings, more elaborate syntax, and a more discriminative selection from a wider range of words. He makes it clear that both lower-class and middle-class people can make use of either public or formal language patterns; but he suggests that lower-class persons tend to make relatively little use of formal language while middle-class persons can make flexible use of both types. In later papers Bernstein substituted the term *restricted code* for 'public language' and *elaborated code* for 'formal language', and considerably developed his theoretical accounts of the social-class differences in the use of language. Despite the strenuous efforts of Bernstein and his associates to prevent educators from drawing crude inferences from their work, it soon became a widespread belief that lower-class children suffered educationally because the language they possessed was demonstrably inadequate. This led to the notion that socially deprived children should be treated as if they 'had no language at all' and required special programmes of structured lessons on vocabulary and sentence production.[1] This 'deficit hypothesis', as it was called by Bruner and others, has been attacked by many linguists who deny that non-standard dialects lack the formal properties necessary for the expression and communication of thought. All natural languages are equally capable of conveying ideas of great complexity. The work of William Labov with Black American children in New York has sharply confirmed this view: as Labov demonstrated, lower-class speakers do not have such a strong control of certain 'school language' features, but there is no evidence that their language, *as language*, is functionally unsuitable for learning.[2] Whatever may be the disadvantage suffered by lower-class children at school, it is not a necessary or intrinsic quality in their language. This general conclusion has been confirmed by R. K. S. Macaulay's work on language and education in Glasgow.[3]

One of the important distinctions to be made is the difference between competence and performance. Language ability tests measure pupils' actual productions at a given time in given circumstances. This does not necessarily coincide with their competence, what they are capable of doing with language. Children, like all other users of language, vary their linguistic performance with different situations, reacting in accordance with their emotional and purposive reading of each particular situation. Labov found that children who were seen to be inarticulate in a formal interview situation could behave quite differently in situations that were more congenial to them. Bernstein's more recent work makes it clear that the concept of 'restricted code' must not be equated with 'linguistic deprivation'.[4] It is not the case that lower-class children do not have

[1] See for example, C. Bereiter and S. Engelman, *Teaching Disadvantaged Children in the Preschool*, Prentice-Hall, 1966; F. M. Hechinger (ed.), *Pre-School Education Today*, Doubleday, 1966.

[2] W. Labov, *The Study of Nonstandard English*, NCTE, 1969.

[3] R. K. S. Macaulay and G. D. Trevelyan, *Language, Education and Employment in Glasgow*, pub. in typescript by the Scottish Council for Research in Education, 1973.

[4] B. Bernstein, 'A Critique of the Concept of Compensatory Education', in *Education for Democracy*, D. Rubinstein and C. Stoneman (eds), Penguin, 1969.

the linguistic forms in their possession; what seems to handicap them is that they have learned fewer strategies for the use of language. It is a socially specific disadvantage. The school is concerned with making explicit principles and operations in science and the arts, and the lower-class child, unlike the more advantaged middle-class child, has not had the social experience which would make him sensitive to the 'symbolic orders of the school'. Here, perhaps, Bernstein has come together with Bruner in suggesting that it is analytic competence which is required for successful learning in school—particularly at the secondary stage—and that the social circumstances of lower-class families tend to deprive the children of the kind of experience which makes for competence in thinking and language use. It is widely believed that socially (and 'culturally') deprived children do not have adequate language and social experience in their homes to enable them to cope with the demands made on them by the school. How these disadvantages can be compensated for is the concern of many recent and current educational projects, such as the Headstart programmes in the USA, the EPA programmes in Britain, home visitor schemes and such projects as the 'Talk Reform' project by the Gahagans, the Schools Council Swansea project, and Dr Joan Tough's project at Leeds. All of these projects represent what the Report (5.30) calls 'planned intervention in the child's language development'.

It has been argued, however, that it is simply social convention that requires the 'elaborated code' in school, and that children who do not use it suffer educationally because they fail to reach up to their teachers' expectations.[1] If this is the case, it is in the teacher that change should be effected: teachers should avoid basing their evaluation of pupils' competence solely on the basis of their speech patterns. Much more powerfully, it can be suggested that lower-class children can, in the right circumstances, manipulate concepts very skilfully even in the 'restricted code' and in their 'subcultural' dialect. The 'language deficit' view may therefore owe something to middle-class social bias. The linguistic differences described by Bernstein may simply be differences of *style* or *register* within dialects. Lower-class children are less accustomed to using the more formal registers employed in school.

Registers are varieties of language used in different social contexts. They can be characterized in various ways. In *The Five Clocks* Joos[2] employs a five-point scale of style: frozen—formal—consultative—casual—intimate. More recently, scholars have distinguished between formal and colloquial registers, casual and ceremonial, personal and impersonal, simple and complex.[3] A particular register can be described for any field of discourse: thus it is possible to distinguish

[1] Peter Trudgill, *Sociolinguistics*, Penguin, 1975.
[2] M. Joos, *The Five Clocks*, Bloomington, Indiana, 1962.
[3] Geoffrey Leech, *English in Advertising*, Longman, 1966.

the linguistic features of, for example, a 'scientific' register, or a 'legal' register, or the register of the classroom. Clearly effective discourse requires the selection of the most suitable register features for a given situation. Similarly, in successful writing we adopt the stylistic conventions which best suit our intentions and the various criteria we set up for particular purposes.

Children who have access to a narrow range of stylistic options will suffer educational disadvantage, and so long as the more formal styles are the only ones accepted in the classroom, lower-class children will be penalized. A similar penalty is meted out to speakers of non-SE dialects. There is a widespread belief that SE contains a God-given code of rules and that any variation from it represents an intrinsically inferior form of the language. Linguists have demonstrated that this is not true. No variety of English is *linguistically* inferior to any other in the sense that it is less effective in carrying meaning, or less beautiful or less complex or less consistent in its rules of grammar, lexis and style. Teachers who condemn the nonstandard speech of the West Indian or Glaswegian or Cockney child are merely confusing their social or racial bias with their linguistic misconceptions.[1]

Language functions

In a brilliant and influential paper written for educators, M. A. K. Halliday suggests that the child who, in Bernstein's terms, uses a 'restricted code' is one who has failed to master the operation of certain language functions. 'The "restriction" is a restriction on the range of uses of language'.[2] In this and subsequent works, Halliday has provided us with a comprehensive view of the relationships between language and the social situations in which language is used. Each situation in which linguistic interaction occurs can be described structurally in terms of the general categories of *field*, *tenor*, and *mode*. *Field* is the type of activity going on—the social 'subject-matter' as it were. *Tenor* is the role relationships, how the participants are interacting with one another. *Mode* is the rhetorical function assigned to language in a particular type of situation—for example, whether spoken or written, whether the speech is informal or not, and so on. An utterance or text is linguistically determined by the field, tenor and mode of the situation: that is, the choice of meanings,

---

[1] P. Trudgill, *op. cit.*, p. 57ff.
[2] M. A. K. Halliday, 'Relevant Models of Language', in *The State of Language*, Univ. of Birmingham, 1969.

and hence the lexical and grammatical properties of the utterance or text are called upon to fit the situation.[1]

Halliday suggests that children internalize 'models' of language as a result of their experience of using language in different situations. 'The determining elements in the young child's experience are the successful demands on language that he himself has made. . . . Language is, for the child, a rich and adaptable instrument for the realization of his intentions; there is hardly any limit to what he can do with it'.[2] He proposes the following typology of the language models with which normal children are endowed:

INSTRUMENTAL. This is the simplest model, the use of language as 'a means of getting things done', for the satisfaction of personal material needs: serving the 'I want' function.

REGULATORY. The use of language as a means of regulating the behaviour of others, serving the function of 'Do as I tell you'.

INTERACTIONAL. This model refers to the use of language for maintaining and mediating one's relationships with others: serving the 'me and him' (or 'me and Mummy') function.

PERSONAL. This is the model which enables the child to express his own individuality: serving the 'Here I come' function.

HEURISTIC. This model refers to language as a means of finding out, questioning: serving the function 'Tell me why'.

IMAGINATIVE. This model enables the child to project himself into an environment of his own making, to create a world of make-believe: serving the 'Let's pretend' function.

REPRESENTATIONAL. This is the use of language as a means of conveying information and expressing propositions: serving the function of 'I've got something to tell you'.

These are not models of language acquisition, nor are they psychological or pedagogical categories; they are merely some of the functions language can perform, ways in which children can be seen to operate with language. In another sense, they are illustrations of the great variety of the uses of language, and for the educator this is the chief importance of Halliday's analysis. Teachers ought to be aware of the many ways in which language is used in social intercourse and in the course of the individual's life. Again, recalling the work of Piaget and Bruner, we must realize the importance of founding teaching procedures on the child's existing knowledge and experience, enabling him to make new experience compatible with what he already knows. Also, we must as educators be sensitive to the *unnatural* as well as the *natural* varieties of language-use: that is, the fact that some capabilities cannot be left to maturational processes. Halliday's *personal* and *heuristic* functions, both crucial to educational success, will only become familiar through planned experience and training.

[1] M. A. K. Halliday, 'Talking One's Way In: A Sociolinguistic Perspective on Language and Learning', in *Problems of Language and Learning*, Davies, A. (ed.), Heinemann Educational, 1975.
[2] 'Relevant Models of Language', *op. cit.*

Piaget's concept of 'formal operations', Bruner's concept of 'analytic competence', Bernstein's concept of 'elaborated code' and Halliday's concept of language models are all separately conceived entities of different theoretical frameworks, and we ought not to confuse or equate them: at the same time, they constitute powerful demonstrations from different disciplines of the existence of a way of using thought processes and language which must be the ultimate goal set for every pupil.

Another approach to the study of language functions arises from the interest of scholars such as J. L. Austin[1] and J. R. Searle[2] in discourse analysis. This is based upon a consideration of the *speech act*. An utterance is never merely a sentence: saying something purposively is an action, the intention being to produce some effect on the person addressed. For example, to say 'I promise (something)' is not merely to tell the hearer something: it *is promising*. Such *performative* utterances have meaning related to the speech situation as well as the meaning of their propositional content. Austin points out that an utterance has an 'illocutionary force' over and above its locutionary content. If I am trying to tell you something, I have succeeded in telling it as soon as you have perceived what it is I am trying to tell you. There are 'rules of use' which relate *what is said* to *what is performed*. The theory of discourse analysis is relatively new, and it is as much a philosophical concern as a linguistic one; but it has provided valuable insights into the functioning of language.

The way language is used in the classroom has become an important study for a number of educators.[3] Douglas Barnes, for example, has analysed classroom interaction in terms of the types of questions asked and answers elicited, the types of responses made to different initiating utterances and instructions, the relationship between the teacher's instructional language and the pupils' understanding and so on. Clearly children in the classroom have to learn the 'rules of use' to enable them to cope with their learning tasks. Sinclair and his associates have produced an elaborate analysis of classroom discourse, which has resulted from a fruitful combination of discourse analysis and interaction analysis (that is, the classification of verbal interchanges between teacher and pupils).

Sinclair establishes a hierarchy of discourse units: the *lesson*, the *transaction*, the *exchange*, the *move*, and the *act*, each unit consisting of combinations of the smaller units. The units are described linguistically in terms of Halliday's scale and category grammar. The units

[1] J. L. Austin, *How to Do Things with Words*, Clarendon Press, 1962.
[2] J. R. Searle, *Speech Acts*, OUP, 1969.
[3] See, for example, D. Barnes, J. Britton and H. Rosen, *Language, the Learner and the School*, Penguin, 1971; J. W. P. Creber, *Lost for Words: Language and Educational Failure*, Penguin, 1972; C. Rosen and H. Rosen, *The Language of Primary School Children*, Penguin, 1973; J. Sinclair, *et al.*, *The English Used by Teachers and Pupils*, Univ. of Birmingham, 1972.

at the lowest rank of discourse are called *acts*, which have functional properties and would seem to resemble what Austin means by 'speech acts'. This analysis makes available, for the first time, a descriptive framework for further research into how language operates in teaching and learning.

Usage

It has been said that using language is rule-governed behaviour. But many people tend to confuse the rules of grammar with the conventions of style. The rules and conventions of linguistic usage have preoccupied rhetoricians and grammarians for centuries; but recent studies have revealed that many widely held notions of what is 'correct' in usage are confused and confusing.

W. H. Mittins has pointed out various kinds of 'rule' invoked by various 'authorities'. There is the 'ipsedixitism': the rule that something is so because someone has said so with authority. Examples of this are the *shall/will* convention pronounced by Wallis in the seventeenth century; and Bishop Lowth's decision that *than* was always a conjunction and not a preposition and so must be followed by a nominative pronoun. Then there is the appeal to Latin. Latin was used as a model for the grammatical description of English, and seventeenth- and eighteenth-century grammarians also derived 'rules' for English usage from Latin. Thus Dryden condemned the use of a preposition as the last word in a sentence because in Latin prepositions are preposed. Then there is the appeal to '*logic*'; for example by those who deplore the use of *aggravate* for *annoy* because the word incorporates the Latin *gravis* and must therefore always mean 'make worse'.[1] The truth is that in usage there is no single standard of acceptability available to us; there are multiple standards.[2] What may be adjudged 'wrong' at one time may be widely accepted at another; what may be pronounced 'barbarous' or 'inelegant' by a self-styled authority may be universally used and tolerated in everyday practice; what may be urged as 'correct' in one part of the English-speaking world may be wholly ignored in another.

Some teachers are prone to confuse 'correctness' with 'desirableness': to lay down prescriptions as to what is proper in speech or writing, and to emphasize prescriptive 'rules'. *Don't's* often predominate over *do's* in traditional course books, and pupils are expected to be able to rationalize the cause of 'error' in terms of the 'rules'.

[1] W. H. Mittin, 'What is Correctness?', in *The State of Language*, A. Wilkinson (ed.), Univ. of Birmingham, 1969.

[2] See R. Quirk (ed.), *The Use of English*, Longman, 1962.

Many of these proscribed forms are common in the everyday speech of SE speakers: such forms, for example, as *It's me, Each of them have taken one, Who did you say you gave it to?* are universally employed in informal SE. It is absurd to suggest that they are erroneous in ordinary speech, though they would not normally occur in formal written English. The 'Correction of Errors' exercises characteristic of many old-fashioned textbooks exemplify this confusion between what is 'correct' in formal composition and what is normal in informal conversation. To require a pupil to 'correct' such sentences as 'Excuse me being late', 'I rose late so I had to hurry', 'The man only died yesterday', and 'Who did you come with?' is to misunderstand the difference between the uses of language in different situations.[1] These sentences are colloquial; they would seldom occur in the kind of prose in which the 'rules' they are thought to err against are relevant. The truth is that different styles of English require different conventions, not only of phonology and grammar and lexis, but also of meaning. There is no sense in setting pupils to 'correct' such sentences as those cited here, since they are all correct enough in appropriate contexts. They might be 'translated' into different registers or styles, but in the process of translation they will probably take on different meanings. It is worth remembering, too, that a number of so-called solecisms—such as the split infinitive, and the use of a terminal preposition—are quite frequent in the writing of our best authors. Taking liberties with conventions is a well-known characteristic of literary writing.

There is, then, no ineluctable or transcendental measure of correctness in any form of language. What is 'right' in any situation or task is what is most appropriate. The idea of correctness must yield to that of appropriateness, of suitability, as the most useful basis for judgements of the quality of effectiveness of language. The language that best fits the needs of the speaker or writer, the situation, the subject at hand, is the 'right' language. This is not to say that there is never a right–wrong opposition. Of course there are many occasions when it is possible to say, unreservedly, that one form is wrong and another is right. But it is necessary to distinguish between different levels of subjectivity in judgement making, with different ranges of acceptability. In the technical sense 'grammaticality' affords yes/no judgements which few native speakers would question. Where situational criteria operate a form can only be judged suitable by reference to the context. In matters of style our judgements are made by reference to our notions of what is 'adequate' or 'effective' or 'acceptable'. In questions of usage the only recourse we have is to what is generally deemed to be 'acceptable'.

---

[1] A. M. Philp, *Attitudes to Correctness in English*, Longman, 1968.

Grammar and education

The word *grammar* has several different connotations. Historically, *grammar* has meant the whole linguistic apparatus of a people, their speech and mainly their writings. To the modern linguistics scholar the grammar of a language is the organization of its words in sentences, its morphology and syntax. In education *grammar* has often been taken to indicate what is 'right' and 'wrong' in the use of language. Finally, a *grammar* can be taken to indicate a statement of how a language works. In modern educational circles distinctions are made between *traditional grammar*, *structural grammar*, Hallidayan or *scale and category grammar*, and Chomskyan or *transformational–generative grammar*.

Traditional grammar developed from the study of Greek and Latin grammars by such scholars as Aelius Donatus, whose fourth-century *Ars Grammatica* described Latin in terms of the eight parts of speech. A long scholarly tradition of grammatical studies, from the sixteenth to the early twentieth centuries, applied Latin grammatical concepts such as *tense*, *case*, and *voice* to the European languages, and a large number of reference grammars was produced for English, French, German and other European languages. Grammars of 'newly discovered' African and Asian languages were compiled, and by the beginning of this century a massive volume of technical information had been gathered for most of the known languages. Early in the century three great grammars were produced within this scholarly tradition: Henrik Poutsma's *Grammar of Late Modern English*, Etsko Kruisinga's *Handbook of Present-day English*, and Otto Jespersen's *Modern English Grammar on Historical Principles*.[1]

The school grammar drawn from this traditional corpus tended to concentrate on the parsing of words (*parsing* derives from *pars*, 'part' of speech), the analysis of complex sentences into clause-types and of 'simple' or one-clause sentences into Subject–Predicate–Object/Complement parts. Each part of speech was defined on a notional basis, according to its generalized 'meaning' and 'function'. Thus a *noun* was 'the name of an object, person or thing', a verb was a 'doing word', an adjective a 'describing word' and so on. Sentences were classified as simple, compound, complex, and compound-complex, and clause-types were categorized as independent and subordinate, each subordinate clause being defined functionally as adjectival, adverbial, nominal and so on. The rationale of the teaching of grammar in this way was largely utilitarian, since it was believed that an understanding of sentence structure would lead to more competent writing; but there was an idealistic aspect, too, as many educators firmly believed that the study of grammar developed a mental discipline which would transfer to other learning activities.

[1] H. A. Gleason, Jr, *Linguistics and English Grammar*, Holt, Rinehart & Winston, 1965.

There were many pedagogical objections to school grammar teaching during the 1920s and 1930s, and by the end of the Second World War most progressive educators were convinced that it was largely a waste of time. Research was demonstrating that there was little or no transfer of training to the pupils' productive language, either in speech or writing.[1] Much of the so-called 'grammar' in text books, moreover, consisted of dull and unprofitable exercises, such as the correction of 'Common Errors' and prescriptive 'rules' of composition and prosody.

At this time, too, structural linguists in America were criticizing traditional grammar from a linguistic viewpoint. They argued that a grammar based on Latin could not be valid for English, since the two languages are 'essentially, basically, radically different'.[2] The languages are certainly dissimilar in their methods of organizing linguistic substance: Latin is highly inflectional while English is mainly distributive (that is, the English sentence relies more on word-order than on the inflection of words). The linguists criticized traditional grammarians' reliance on notional categories for defining the elements of the sentence, and demonstrated that it often fails. (For instance, if a noun is 'the name of something' and a verb 'denotes an action', is *dictation* a noun or a verb or both?) They criticized the traditional scholars' exclusive interest in the written language—this itself as a term is a misnomer to the structuralist, who equates language with speech and regards writing as 'speech written down'. They also criticized the prevalent school grammar for being preoccupied by false notions of correctness and by prescriptive and proscriptive rules.

Structural linguistics produced a 'new grammar' of English and other languages. This was scientifically worked out as an analysis of the sentence into 'immediate constituents' (ICs) or 'pattern parts'. For example, the sentence *The three old ladies upstairs own a boxer dog with a mean temper* can be broken down into various pairs of constituents, each pair consisting of lesser parts until the minimal meaningful linguistic elements are reached.[3] Thus the sentence can be cut into two ICs:

The three old ladies upstairs	own a boxer dog with a mean temper
NOMINAL GROUP	VERBAL GROUP

The verbal group can be cut into

own   a boxer dog with a mean temper

[1] See, for example, W. J. Macaulay, 'The difficulty of grammar', in *British Journal of Educational Psychology*, 1947, 17, pp. 153–162.

[2] Charlton Laird, *Thinking About Language*, Holt, Rinehart & Winston, 1961.

[3] This example is taken from Gleason, *op. cit.*, Chapter 7.

All the constituents of the sentence can be shown by means of a 'tree diagram' thus:

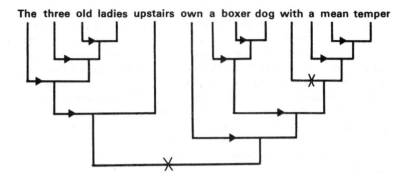

The three old ladies upstairs own a boxer dog with a mean temper

Grammatical descriptions of a structuralist type were produced by C. C. Fries, Harold Whitehall, Paul Roberts and others in the USA and by Randolph Quirk, Barbara Strang and W. H. Mittins in Britain.[1] Apart from the sentence analyses which the 'new linguistics' offered there was also a considerable revision of the grammatical terminology of the traditionalists, and some educational grammarians (for instance, Whitehall and Roberts) proposed a quite novel set of terms for use in schools. Although some of the grammatical work of the structuralist school has been superseded during the last decade, much of the writing contained important scholarship and some of the books, in particular those of Fries, Quirk and Strang, are still to be highly recommended for their valuable insights into the nature of the English language.

M. A. K. Halliday's 'scale and category grammar', now developed into a full-scale systemic grammar of English, has been much studied by British educators. Halliday proposes a taxonomy of units: *sentence, clause, phrase* (or *group*), *word* and *morpheme*. Thus a sentence can be shown to consist of one or more clauses, a clause of one or more phrases, a phrase of one or more words, and a word of one or more morphemes. This is the *rank scale*, and a unit can be seen at times to operate at a different rank from its usual one. Thus in the sentence *The man I saw ran away* the noun phrase *The man I saw* contains a *rank-shifted* clause, *I saw*: that is to say, *I saw* would normally be a clause but in this sentence it is part of a noun phrase, the unit below it in the rank scale. The notion of rank-shift is an illuminating one,

---

[1] C. C. Fries, *The Structure of English*, Harcourt Brace, 1952; H. Whitehall, *Structural Essentials of English*, Longman, 1958; P. Roberts, *Patterns of English*, Harcourt Brace, 1956; *ibid.*, *English Sentences*, Harcourt Brace, 1962; R. Quirk, *The Use of English*, Longman, 1962; B. Strang, *Modern English Structure*, Arnold, 1962; W. H. Mittins, *A Grammar of Modern English*, Methuen, 1962.

particularly for deepening our understanding of the relationship between syntax and logical meaning.

Halliday also proposes a category of *structure* which enables us to identify the structural elements of a sentence. The structural labels S, P, C, and A, can be glossed as Subject-place, Predicator-place, Complement-place and Adjunct-place, and a number of grammar study programmes have been produced for teachers on this basis.[1] This is an 'Immediate Constituents' type of sentence analysis, but where the structural linguist employs a binary-division process the Hallidayan linguist will employ a multiple-division process. According to Currie, the 'many ICs model is simple to use in class, can lead on to much more profound statements about language than mere identification of elements in places; it can also form part of a functional approach to language, which has always received the support of education'.[2]

Chomsky's transformational-generative (known as TG) grammar presupposes, as we have seen, that a grammar must be able to account for all the grammatical sentences possible to produce in a language. His grammatical model therefore specifies the grammatical rules required for constructing sentences. The words and morphemes of a sentence are arranged in functional constituents such as subject, predicate, object and so on, and a speaker's knowledge of this internal structure can be represented (in part, at least) by means of 'phrase structure' rules.

The first of these rules is simply that a sentence can consist of a noun phrase followed by a verb phrase, and the rule is represented thus:

$$S \longrightarrow NP + VP$$

(The arrow is an instruction to 'rewrite' the left-hand symbol as the string of symbols which follow it.)

Other rules tell us that *NP* can be rewritten as *Art*+*N* (since a noun phrase can be rewritten as *boy, table, Johnson* etc; that *Art* can be rewritten *as a, an,* or *the*; that *VP* can be rewritten as *Aux*+*V* (since a verb phrase can consist of an auxiliary and a main verb); that *Aux* can be rewritten as *can, may, will, should,* etc., and so on. Thus we can list some grammatical rules:

1	S	NP+VP
2	NP	Art+N
3	VP	Aux+V+NP
4	Aux	(can, may, will, should, etc.)

---

[1] See W. B. Currie, *New Directions in Teaching English Language*, Longman, 1973. This is an excellent short account of current school grammars and their development.

[2] W. B. Currie, *op. cit.*, 45.

5 V   (walk, hit, kick, explain, etc.)
6 Art   (a, an, the)
7 N   (boy, table, Johnson, ball, etc.)

We can now construct a *derivation* of a sentence by rewriting the left-hand symbol with the elements on the right-hand. For example, the sentence *The boy will kick the ball* yields the following derivation:

S
NP+VP (by rule 1)
Art+N+VP (by rule 2)
Art+N+Aux+V+NP (by rule 3)
Art+N+Aux+V+art+N (by rule 2)
the+boy+will+kick+the+ball (by rules 4, 5, 6, 7)

This derivation can be represented by a *tree diagram*:

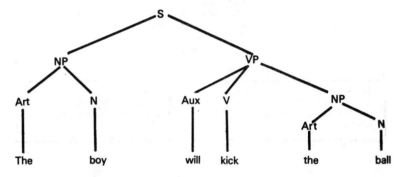

This 'phrase marker' is the TG representation of the syntax of one sentence. (Chomsky is not, of course, suggesting that a speaker consciously or unconsciously applies these rules in his mind. The rules merely represent 'internalized' rules that are implicit in the grammar.)

Phrase structure rules can be shown to underlie the *kernel* or basic sentences in English. Chomsky points out, however, that phrase structure rules can only generate a partial grammar to cater for a mere fragment of English. In addition to these rules, the grammar requires *transformational* rules which transform phrase markers into other phrase markers by adding or deleting or rearranging elements. The basic rules generate the 'deep structure' of a sentence; the transformational rules change the deep structure into the 'surface structure'. There are many transformational rules: for converting active to passive, or singular to plural, for rearranging the elements of a sentence, and so on. It is the transformational rules which account for the ambiguity of such a sentence as *I like her cooking*. It can be shown that several different basic sentences yield this same phrase marker: for example, *I like what she cooks, I like the way she cooks,*

I like the fact that she cooks etc. Different transformational rules convert the different basic sentences into the same 'surface' sentence.[1]

In addition to transformational rules, a TG grammar employs *morphographemic* rules, which convert the various morphemes into the form of written words, and *morphophonetic* rules, which convert the morphemes into their phonological representations. The Chomskyan theory can be graphically described by a simplified model:

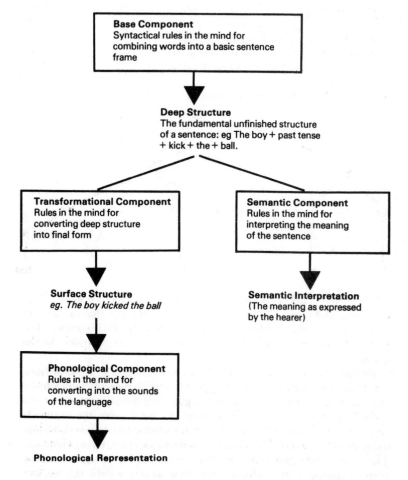

Chomsky's preoccupation with syntax has been attacked by a new school of 'generative semanticists' who argue that meaning and syntax are intertwined: the grammar starts with a description of the meaning of a sentence, and then generates the syntactical

[1] This example is taken from an article by John Searle in a Special Supplement of the *New York Review*, 29 June, 1972.

structure by means of syntactical and lexical rules. They postulate a 'semantic component': rules in the mind for generating the structural frame of a sentence and its meaning simultaneously. The theory of generative semantics is relatively new, but the growing modern interest in the relation between syntax and semantics may well have implications of some importance for our understanding of how a grammar works.

The concept of deep and surface grammar is present also in Halliday's consideration of *system*. This category concerns the options which operate in the selection of the forms realized in a particular structure. Three systems operate on the clause. The system of *transitivity* concerns the 'actor', the 'process' and the 'goal' as functions in a clause. Thus in the sentence, *Sir Christopher Wren built this gazebo*, the 'actor' function is realized by *Sir Christopher Wren*, the 'process' function by *built* and the 'goal' function by *this gazebo*. The system of *Mood* concerns the speech functions of the clause, and the options which allow a speaker to vary his role in communicating with others in social interaction. Such speech functions as making statements, asking questions, uttering orders and making exclamations are expressed grammatically by the *mood* system. The system of *Theme* concerns the organization of the clause as a message. The English clause consists of a 'theme'—the 'psychological subject', the peg on which the message is hung—and a 'rheme', which is the 'new' information. Thus in *I don't know*, *I* is the theme and *don't know* is the rheme; in *Suddenly the rope gave way*, *Suddenly* is the theme and the rest of the utterance is the rheme.[1]

It will be obvious from this very brief and simplified account of modern grammars that we now have a comprehensive body of descriptive matter for discussing the structures of sentences, and educationalists have not been slow in attempting to make use of it for teaching purposes. Both Chomsky and Halliday have exerted great influence on educational thinking, not only by providing sources for pedagogical grammars but also by providing insights into the operation of language in thinking and communication. In America, Chomsky's work has been extensively misapplied. The term 'generative' has been widely misinterpreted and associated erroneously with educational notions like 'creative writing' and 'productive learning' and Chomsky has himself warned educators that he sees little direct relevance to schooling in his TG grammar. In Britain, Halliday has openly interested himself in education, and has written several seminal papers on the educational implications of his work, particularly in the sociolinguistic field. As W. B. Currie puts it: 'Bloomfield took a destructive and even a vicious attitude to school language work; Chomsky has been marked by a studied agnosticism on the question of application. Halliday has maintained a steady and

[1] M. A. K. Halliday, 'Language Structure and Language Function', in *New Horizons in Linguistics*, J. Lyons (ed.), Penguin, 1970.

fruitful contact with educational programmes for over a decade'.[1]

The place of grammar in the classroom has been diminished during the last half-century because the traditional pedagogical grammar was thought to be deficient, but also because teachers lost faith in grammar work as a source of training in the use of language. Modern English teaching begins with the belief that you best learn English through using it, and our concentration on the productive involvement of children in practical language-using situations is unquestionably justified. The language-acquisition paradigm described by modern psycholinguistics suggests that the development of linguistic skills as children mature will best occur if they are continuously experimenting with language in live or simulated interaction with other users of language: that is, by engaging in talk, reading and writing in contexts which motivate the active interchange of ideas. The importance of such practice is so great that efficient teachers rightly resist any activity which may compete for the time required, especially when they cannot fully accept that the activity is genuinely useful.

At the same time, all pupils must acquire a set of linguistic concepts and terms. Whether he wants to or not, every teacher is engaged in transmitting notions about language all the time he is teaching. The teacher is rightly concerned with language production and the systematic teaching of a pedagogical grammar, however modern, however 'respectable' in its linguistic conception, cannot be regarded as productive in this sense. Since native speakers of English acquire a grammatical competence intuitively, the methodical description of grammar, along with the procedures of analysis, cannot be justified in terms of results, and the time given to it would be better employed in other language activities.[2]

With children in the primary school, grammatical terminology of a minimal kind may be occasionally useful, for example in advising pupils about their writing of sentences and so on; but in practice teachers need do little more than draw attention to generalizations emerging from the children's own knowledge.[3] With older pupils in the secondary school, the teacher should, however, be prepared to use grammatical knowledge more explicitly, since the discussion of texts, whether in reading or the pupils' own writing, requires descriptive terms—what linguists call a 'metalanguage'—for talking about language. This implies that teachers—of all subjects—should be sufficiently familiar with the terms and concepts of modern linguistic analysis to enable them to speak usefully about the language used in pupils' work. That there is no room for formal grammar

[1] W. B. Currie, *op. cit.*, p. 52.
[2] *The Teaching of English Language*, Bulletin No. 5 of the (Scottish) Central Committee on English, HMSO, 1972.
[3] *Children and Their Primary Schools* (Plowden Report), HMSO, 1967, p. 222.

teaching does not mean that there is no need for teachers to know something about grammar. There is a good case for the acquisition of grammatical knowledge by all teachers, so that they can convey to their pupils the linguistic insights which improve efficiency in the use of language at all stages and for all purposes.

It is of course, the teacher of English to whom we look for the major contribution in language teaching. Even in the English classroom, however, formal grammar has little justification. The English teacher must, of course, pay particular attention to his pupils' use of language, devising the means to promote competence and to motivate study and practice. English teachers should know a great deal about grammars and grammatical theory. They should be able, when they see the need, to give their pupils illustrated explanations to show the value of particular applications of rules and conventions — thus they should be capable of giving lessons on grammar in order to explicate a point of style, or to show how common errors can be understood and avoided, or to give the pupils guidance as to how they can construct more effective sentences. All of these activities are better thought of as *rhetoric*, the art of composition; but they require grammatical analysis to be properly appreciated. And since the metalanguage cannot be learned by pupils in the course of a systematized programme of grammar work, the teacher should take every opportunity that arises to use the terms which facilitate reference to linguistic features. This is the process of 'mention'; the gradual conveying of a body of terminology as the need for terms arises. Through 'mention', which of course involves much sophisticated knowledge and skill in the teacher, the pupils will in time acquire a vocabulary for talking about language which will enable them to work with language at a mature level.

The teacher of foreign languages requires a thorough knowledge of the grammar of the languages he teaches, and his competence will be greater if his operational knowledge is founded on a good understanding of grammatical theory. Traditionally, modern language teachers have looked to their English colleagues to give pupils a 'grounding' in English grammar on which they can work. This is not now a legitimate expectation, since it is not necessary for pupils to have formal grammar in the English classroom. Modern linguists have turned, of course, to oral methods, but even so many feel it desirable to employ some grammatical description. Where this is the case, the foreign language teacher must provide the information himself; and it is to be hoped that he will be able to make use of the work of linguistics scholars. Almost everything that Chomsky, Halliday and others say about English applies to French, German, Russian and other modern languages. The process of 'mention' and the spot lesson to illustrate a process or a construction, can be as effective in foreign language teaching as in English.

The teacher of Latin can also benefit from a knowledge of modern grammatical theory. New Latin pedagogical grammars have been produced, some of which purport to introduce patterns more systematically than the traditional textbooks did. More importantly, perhaps, the very dissimilarity between the grammars of Latin and English suggests that secondary school pupils with an academic turn of mind could benefit from a specially devised course of grammatical study designed to give them an understanding of 'universal' grammar. Taught properly, a course in Latin could lead to knowledge of the systems and categories of grammar which, besides being interesting in its own right, could provide a good basis for the study of modern languages.

PART II

The Components of a Policy

4. The Teachers' Approach

An attitude to language

Because access to so much learning is through language, and because the very process of understanding involves verbalizing, that is because learning is operating with language, it is clearly important that all teachers have an outline idea of the fundamentals of how language works. Whatever our specialist function in education we work with language, and we must, as individuals and as a school team, have a common attitude towards our most precious skill. And yet this is not easy for a number of reasons.

In the first place many people's ideas about language, what it is and how it works, are folk lore with very little basis in truth; indeed frequently they are misleading. This is not surprising as most of the research studies into the nature of language, which Dr Gatherer outlined in Chapter 3, are fairly recent. The findings of the linguists from the 'twenties onwards have not yet filtered down into everyday educated knowledge. Most professional people know far more about economics, sociology, or the internal combustion engine than they do about language.

Further, language is very personal, and it is difficult for all but the linguistic specialist to find ways of talking about language, which, of course, means talking about *oneself*, without becoming personal, embarrassed, touchy, or upset. It is easier for us to talk about the technicalities of, say, teaching with audio-visual aids than our use of language in the classroom. I fear that this aspect of a suggested language policy may seem daunting: if linguistics is such a deep, difficult, and disputable study, what can the ordinary teacher usefully learn of it? Yet Dr Gatherer has shown the agreed central truths, and his six generalizations on page 35 are the foundations of a teacher's and a school's approach to working with language. I would suggest that a school could use those six statements as a basis for considering language in the school.

Perhaps the most fundamental linguistic point for educators is that language 'is a means of categorizing and ordering human experience' (Dr Gatherer's phrase). Therefore people who teach those subject areas concerned with the analysis and categorization of experience need to realize that they are not merely using language as an expository device: the pupil must re-use it to achieve the categorizing and ordering that is the intellectual heart of the sciences, the humanities, and even mathematics.

For the teacher the 'arbitrary', 'selected', 'conventional' nature of the symbols of language means that attention and the establishment of criteria for helping pupils must be directed at how language is used in the society we are preparing our pupils for. Attempts to establish 'natural or inevitable' meanings are artificial. A knowledgeable and reasonably sensitive attitude to language is, I suspect, likely to encourage the school to teach specific skills, rather than to attempt to make the pupil into the teacher's own image.

Dr Gatherer's point about language and thought should permeate the pastoral and curricular life of the school: he points out that the idea of language as the 'clothing of thought', is less useful than considering it as the 'embodiment of thought'. That being so, we cannot offer language forms ('Energy is...', 'A ritual is...', 'Symmetry is...') 'off the peg' for the pupil to don and use. The pupil must come to the understanding through exploratory language.

I shall take four aspects of thinking about language, and show how teaching practices might be affected by this attitude.

English as a distributive language

Perhaps the central technical point about our language is that it is essentially a *distributive* language; that is, sense comes out of the connections between words. In an inflected language the connections are shown by changes in the actual words; in an uninflected language by the word order, or distribution.

The normal English word order is very deeply embedded in our minds:

The man hit the boy.

We all know exactly what this means, and if 'boy' and 'man' are transposed the meaning alters. In an inflected language, word order is far less important for sense because it is obvious whether the boy did the hitting or the man according to the inflected ending. Thus the distributive nature of our language, and its consequent dependence on word order, is far more important than inflection.

Yet schools tend to be more interested in the more easily noted, and thus 'corrected' inflectional oddities of a pupil than in helping pupils towards making more of word order. A school pondering this might consider scrutinizing examples of pupil's talk and writing to establish if word order could be profitably worked on.

The vocabulary

Both a strength and a difficulty of our language is its immense and immensely varied vocabulary. 'The vernacular of vernaculars', as Robert Graves called it, has grown from 'the lingo used between the

Norman-French conquerors and their Anglo-Saxon serfs', and kept the resulting diversity of vocabulary. We have, for instance, an unusually wide choice of prefixes of different origins. We have also a number of near alternative words, but each with particular associations and uses. Never watched over by an academy, constantly added to as we borrowed from other languages, our vocabulary allows a richly personal use, but only to those who are at ease with it. Spelling conventions are particularly difficult, a problem which goes back to the post-conquest time when there was a long period during which spelling patterns did not settle down. The spelling difficulties which trouble pupils should be seen not merely as requiring surface tidying, but as a problem central to their gradual exploration of this large vocabulary.

If we ponder the nature of our vocabulary and its system, we realize that a school as a whole must have a conscious plan to help pupils throughout their school years, a plan which will be both specific and contextual. Much of Chapter 6 will be devoted to the kinds of practical policies that might grow from this consideration.

Notions of appropriateness

In our anxiety not to be sloppy, and in our own nervousness about language, we sometimes push rules which are inappropriate for the occasion, are too early for the pupils' growing approximations, or are even entirely wrong: that is, they just do not exist. I am not alleging that because on an off day in a casual piece of writing a well-known writer uses a particular form that it is acceptable. I am suggesting that some rules exist only in schoolrooms. Dr Gatherer has nicely balanced the necessary objectivity with the equally necessary need to learn ' "rules of use" in social situations' and ' "rules of effectiveness" in communication'.

In establishing a language policy, a staff might need to explore the difference between accepting everything and giving positive help. Some teachers in a rash of conscientiousness endeavour to prune and shape pupils' language into what they take to be acceptable. Let us consider some of the wrong-headed reasons which are sometimes advanced by teachers, and which a language policy should clarify.

'Laziness' is one of the commonest explanations, as well as criticisms, of socially less prestigious pronunciations. A moment's thought, however, challenges this. The 'dropped' 't' in 'butter' can be dubbed 'lazy' only by those who forget that it is acceptable, indeed even 'correct', to leave out the 't' in 'often'. (Fowler criticizes those who pronounce the 't' in 'often' by the label of 'spelling pronunciation'.) Labov looked carefully at stigmatized pronunciation forms and concluded:

> Some of the extreme developments of vernacular vowel shifts in New York City, Detroit, or Chicago are tense vowels which seem to involve a great deal of muscular effort compared to the standard. . . . The usual response is to cite laziness, lack of concern, or isolation from the prestige norm. But

there is no foundation for the notion that stigmatised vernacular forms are easier to pronounce.[1]

'Illogical' or 'ungrammatical', are other justifications for attacking pupils' speech. Teachers who themselves fought to change their grammatical patterns, who learnt the rules of, e.g., subject–verb agreement or of the subjective and objective forms of pronouns, often mis-apply those rules, dubbing alternative *forms* as 'illogical'. It can be, for instance, that the subject form is different from that in standard English. It is not that there are no rules, but that in different forms of speech the rules are met in different ways.

Suffolk speech, for instance, like many other British regional dialects, has different forms for pronouns:

> Us don't want t' play wi' he.
> Oi don't think much o' they.
> Oi went out a-walkin' wi' she.

or in the lovely description of a new schoolmistress by an old Suffolk woman:

> O, har be a buptious botty bitch, har oon't speak t' th' loikes o' we.[2]

There is, of course, perfect language *logic* in the pronoun forms used. It is a consistent pattern, and readily understood. There is certainly no inferiority, still less any confusion or illogicality. The speakers have learnt a grammar which differs from standard English, but which is every bit as grammatical. The school concerned, as it rightly would be, with helping the older pupil cope with the more widely used pronoun patterns would be ill advised, and indeed would be inaccurate, to dub 'he', 'they', 'she', and 'we' as wrong, and to label them nominative forms in objective positions. They are *objective forms* in this grammar, but different objective forms. It ill becomes the teacher to be incorrect in his reason and method of 'correction'.

It is best, I feel, to consider, for instance, West Indian speech only after having given that kind of attention to a mainland dialect. The same points apply: the usual forms are not irregularities; the common phrases, indeed, are not bad grammar. Certainly it is intellectually impossible to analyse the speech as slipshod or illogical. For instance, there will always be subject–verb agreement, and there will always be a consistent use of the appropriate case for pronouns. However, the *form* of verb will differ, as will the form of the pronoun. Here is a West Indian talking:

> I had was to let she think I wouldn't tell he, but, after all, Big Joe and me is friends, and anything I hear 'bout I does tell he, despite the way he does treat me sometimes.

---

[1] William Labov, 'The Study of Language in its Social Context', in *Studium Generale*, Volume 23, 1970, reprinted in J. B. Pride and Janet Holmes (eds), *Sociolinguistics*, Penguin, 1972.

[2] The examples are all taken from A. O. D. Claxton, *The Suffolk Dialect of the Twentieth Century*, Norman Adlard and Company, 1968, p. 11.

The use of 'she' and 'he' is entirely consistent, as is the verbal form 'I does tell', 'he does trust me'.

There is some etymological wrong-headedness amongst teachers who complain about language being spoilt by neologisms, barbarisms, or Americanisms. Too frequently the grounds for the objection are inaccurate. Underlying the whole concern is a false attitude to the language of the past, assuming it to have been a pure one which is being corrupted today. Many of the words being objected to have far more respectable antecedents than the objectors realize. Phrases like 'to meet up with' or 'to make out', which have enjoyed a new lease of life in recent years, in fact started life in this country, in perfectly respectable use, before exportation to America, and a subsequent return home. An example of a usage that has had the full attack of schoolmasterly scorn is the suffix '-wise'. There are many respectable antecedents for this: for example, Bunyan uses 'double-wise' and Coleridge 'maidenwise'.

Of course, this is not to say that we should not be sensitive to usage, and should not have preferences. Nor is the acceptability of a usage in the past evidence of its suitability now. However, we must not (a) attack with inaccurate weapons, substituting fallacious linguistic history for personal taste or for current inappropriateness, and (b) we should consider whether the effort is anyway worth it when the tide of language will take its channels whether individuals try to block it or not. Should we not be using our efforts more positively? As I said in another context, 'the basis of our teaching must be adding, enriching, and encouraging—not deleting, criticizing, inhibiting.'[1]

The 'two languages' theory is another dubious piece of popular linguistic folklore. Its popularity seems to depend on the advocacy of those who have moved socially and economically from less favoured settings and like to feel they still have social and linguistic roots to which they can return. Investigations show that their version of the language they left behind, however warm a feeling it gives them in the bar, is *not* the original, but is nearer their current speech pattern with the insertion of the cruder signals to mark its origin. Labov's careful research makes this quite clear:

> We have not encountered any non-standard speakers who gained good control of a standard language, and still retained control of the non-standard vernacular. . . . Although the speaker may indeed appear to be speaking the vernacular, close examination of his speech shows that his grammar has been heavily influenced by the standard. He may succeed in convincing his listeners that he is speaking the vernacular, but this impression seems to depend upon a number of unsystematic and heavily marked signals.[2]

[1] In an essay 'Mainstream', in Denys Thompson (ed.), *Directions in the Teaching of English*, CUP, 1969, p. 56.
[2] William Labov, *op. cit.*, p. 187.

The class and the locality

Perhaps central to a school's attitude to language will be a consideration of the implications for the secondary school of the theories of
language acquisition and class variations in language. An individual
grows by developing successive approximations to the models he
needs and wishes to acquire. His present language cannot usefully be
regarded as deficient: this would be to encourage the wholly inappropriate beliefs that there are gaps to be filled by offering prepared units
to add to the present form. We know how much harm is done both by
denigrating and over-romanticizing non-standard languages. We
must respect the language the pupil brings with him, and the
language of his home. Our tradition is favourable to the socially less
acceptable forms of speech. Synge listening with relish to the peasants
in the Arran Isles, whose speech was 'like a nut or an apple', is part of
our tradition, as is the peasant poet John Clare. The plays of Shakespeare, are nearer to the vernacular tradition than those of Racine or
Corneille. When these great truths have been in danger of being lost
there has always been someone to remind us. David Holbrook, for
instance in *English for Maturity* and *English for the Rejected*, spoke
eloquently for the power and effectiveness of ordinary speech. His
pleas were absorbed into our system. We may need reminders, but
our educational and cultural tradition, respects the vernacular.

There is an opposite danger: to accept any forms of speech (and
some teachers extend this to obscenities) on all occasions comes from
a mistaken idea that we are thus going out to meet the pupils on their
own ground. A school must relate to its community in a way which
is very subtle, as far as language is concerned. Bullock does stress
that: 'We believe that a child's accent should be accepted, and that
to attempt to suppress it is irrational and neither humane nor necessary.' (10.5) Speaking of 'acceptable standards of grammar and
diction' the Report similarly stresses that: 'The aim is not to alienate
the child from a form of language with which he has grown up.' (10.6)
It is very easy to jump rapidly from these, surely by now unconten-
tious, linguistic recommendations to a simplistic 'anything goes'
approach. From that it is easy to presume that because the local
community does not *use* the speech patterns of standard English,
for local people too 'anything goes'. *The opposite is true*, and a school
that at best wishes to relate to its community and at worst at least
wishes not to offend it must develop a sophisticated understanding of
the local community's expectations. Labov has demonstrated from
careful research evidence[1] that the 'upwardly socially mobile' are
highly sensitive to the sounds of the speakers to whose way of life they
are aspiring. Elsewhere he points out that 'the pattern of subjective
reaction tests shows that those who use the highest percentage of

[1] William Labov, 'Phonological Correlates of Social Stratification', in
American Anthropology, **66**, No. 6 (2), 1964.

stigmatised forms are quickest to stigmatise them in the speech of others'.[1] Labov's work has shown that an urban speech community is not so much a community of people who *speak* in the same way, but one which shares the same prejudice about how others speak. 'Social attitudes are extremely uniform throughout a speech community. . . . In fact it seems plausible to define a speech community as a group of speakers who share a set of social attitudes towards language.'[2] This notion must be respected, incorporated into the school's policy: social *attitudes* are part of the language pattern of the community. Yet educationalists with a great regard for the speech patterns of an area, and a genuine wish to act on that regard, easily become superior and patronizing about the area attitude *towards* speech (and thus to the variations in speech which a speech community has). This is unreal, and indeed dangerous, for it can lead to real breaches with the parent body and with the community.

Conclusion

Underlying any language policy must be some knowledge of language. A school must work out a functional pedagogical understanding of language, and establish an attitude to it. Such an understanding is likely to contain ideas about:

The function of language in life;

How language develops in the young child;

What human beings *do* with language;

The special characteristics of our language, including its vocabulary;

The social context of language;

Notions of appropriateness.

The hardest task is to find ways of working with the pupil's own language, and yet to help him to be able to make his own ideas and ways of thinking which lie outside the scope of that language.

The language of school

I now come to the special question of the language demands of each subject area. Every teaching situation uses language to a considerable extent. Even PE depends on the teacher's explanations, instructions, commands, and encouragement, and the pupils' response to these

[1] William Labov, *op. cit.*, p. 180.
[2] *ibid.*, p. 196.

words. Science, despite all the emphasis on manipulative skills, is essentially based on language. The most obvious way it is used is to carry the subject-teaching of the ostensible curriculum, but *at the same time* there is a hidden curriculum, that in which language itself is being taught. For pupils, knowledge lies out there in shadowy phrases used by the teacher or in dense language printed in books. it is not just that so many of the words are unfamiliar; the way they go together is different too: 'When he tells us to do something, it's OK; I can do it. But when he asks us *about* something, I can't make it out.'

The first problem at school is the sheer quantity of new words and new ways of putting things. As the pupil gets older this accelerates— indeed some attempts to lighten the load for the immediate post-primary years have the effect of making the mid-secondary language incline so steep as to be insurmountable by many. Either way the vocabulary expectations of the new specialized curriculum are very heavy. There also can be devastating language strictures, tight regulations that prevent natural, thoughtful reactions. The English teacher criticizes the use of 'nice' ('Has no meaning. Choose a better description'); the geography teacher will not allow you to describe anywhere as 'beautiful' ('Not the point; you're writing about the land form and the population pattern'); the science teach gets very cross if you say 'I' ('Scientists are objective and impersonal'); the craft teacher is upset if you ask for 'one of those' or 'that' ('You must use the right names; everything's got a name').

The reading material in different subjects is startlingly different, each subject from the other and all from fiction. It is not only the vocabularies that are different. The predominant paragraph patterns are quite different. Mathematics is a startling example. In the last twenty years there has been an increase in the amount of reading offered by and expected by textbooks. (Earlier ones were merely the examples to use after the teacher's explanation.) The language is quite different not only in the use of special terms, but also in the limited and special meanings of ordinary words, such as 'if', 'only', 'all, 'except', 'lot'. The vital difference though, is the almost totally non-redundant and relatively unambiguous language in mathematics. It is arguably the hardest language used in the schools.[1] Other subjects offer other difficulties, where again the problems are terminology, special use of normal words, and density. The logical relationships are tightly packed and difficult to disentangle.

In this passage from a Nuffield reader for middle-secondary school pupils, there are the following difficulties: terminology; sentence structure (three compound adjectives plus 'light' between 'the' and

[1] Considerable research into this has been published in the USA. A readily available and clear analysis by Regine Baron Brunner has been published in this country: 'Reading Mathematical Exposition', in *Educational Research*, Volume 18, No. 3, NFER, June 1976, p. 208.

'bulb'); logical pattern ('Although . . . unfortunately'); important
concept differences embodied in similar words ('effective', 'efficiency'); postponed meaning ('You have only . . . to').

Efficiency
Although the tungsten-filament coiled-coil gas-filled light bulb is effective,
unfortunately it is not very efficient. A high proportion of the electrical
energy that goes into it is transformed into heat. You have only to place
your hand close to it after it has been on for a little while to convince
yourself of this. Then place your hand close to a fluorescent tube which
has been switched on for the same time and judge for yourself how little
heat is being wasted. The difference between the incandescent lamp and
the fluorescent tube will then be obvious. The fluorescent tube has a greater
efficiency—about three times as great.

Even passages that apparently use no difficult terminology actually
offer problems. The concept in the following is quite difficult. The
structure of the last sentence is very difficult, and loses most pupil
readers:

Your experiments have shown that energy very often gets changed into
heat, and that it is possible to change heat into other forms of energy, or
at any rate, to change some of it. The essential thing in any machine that
changes heat into some other form of energy is that some part of the machine
is hotter than all other parts.

In order to grasp the meaning of the second sentence one has to
understand the complement ('that some part of the machine is hotter
than all other parts'), which occurs at the end of the sentence. The
subject ('The essential thing') is separated from the verb ('is') and
the complement by a long descriptive phrase. I call this 'postponed
meaning', a frequent device of expository writing, but very unfamiliar
to the pupil. Teachers often use it in speaking, and I noted the
following start to a sentence said in a classroom:

Another thing we ought to do if we're going to have the folders ready by
the time we've planned (and we need to keep to that so that I can look
through them in time) is . . .

By which time sense is lost to most listeners!
Other science reading is like that in crafts in that it demands two
things at once—reading and doing. At other times, especially in
biological aspects, science books offer a pattern of enumeration or
classification. This can be quite difficult to read. And, of course, all
science writing has a compactness not far short of that in mathematics.
Then there is a range of newly introduced written forms, each fresh,
each abruptly started, and each demanding special conventions:
notes, observations, paragraph answers, essays, which are studied by
Nancy Martin in Chapter 5.

In the classroom there can be a dominance of impersonal language,
so that the linguistic material of the child and his home are thrown
out, and even a false middle-class delicacy introduced. Even more
often, the conventions of a certain form of language are insisted on

too completely and too early. In too many language transactions there is a closed expectation, in which the pupils learn narrowly the kind of expected answer. On other occasions the language is designed primarily to gain group control. Of course, control is necessary in schools, and public language will have to be used in various ways for that control, but care is needed if the control element in language is not to seep into other situations. For instance, a girl was once so conditioned by the control function of language that when the teacher quite genuinely enquired in an English class 'What are you laughing at, Jane?', she automatically responded 'Oh, nothing, Miss' even though the lesson was on a piece of literature in which there was humour and the teacher really wished to discuss what was funny in it.[1] In all these ways there is a real possibility of creating a linguistically alien territory, one in which many of the pupils are continuously baffled. If there is a sink-or-swim attitude, most pupils will, if not sink, at least only just keep afloat.

Analysis shows that the language expectation of some subject specialists is difficult and linguistically remote, and that the reading demands of those subjects are sharply differentiated from experience gained in Primary Schools. This needs to be understood, and the question for staff debate is: what should be done as a response to this knowledge?

The 'left-wing' approach is to solve the problems by dramatically adjusting the language requirements of each subject area: producing simpler reading material, removing special language forms, and trying to make the language experience as like ordinary talk as possible. The 'right-wing' approach is to attempt to teach the pupils how to cope.

Each school must establish its own position. The first is to risk losing real language growth in a variety of valuable extending contexts. The second is to risk total learning failure. Something of each is required —so that the language environment of the subject is not hopelessly daunting and so that the pupil is specifically helped to cope: this is doubly valuable in that it makes the subject learning more effective and gives a fresh language context. A school searching towards a policy is likely to want first to examine the language environment that it has created. To do this a seminar or working party will want to bring together examples of the language presented to pupils at various levels: textbook, worksheets, blackboard transcriptions, tapes of teacher talks. It will then want to discuss and analyse these. Secondly, it will want to consider a similar sample of the language expectations put to the pupils: what are they asked to say and write? (Sections of Chapter 5 discuss these in detail.) This analysis should lead to action of two complementary kinds:

[1] I own this anecdote to Anthony Adams of the Cambridge Institute of Education, together with many good ideas, although, of course, I may have done him an injustice in the recording of them.

1. Alteration of the language environment, either by simplification or by postponement of certain difficulties.
2. Specific help in facing the problems it is agreed to leave in the curriculum. (Most of Chapters 5 and 6 are devoted to suggesting ways.)

Neither course on its own is adequate. Certainly it would be abdication to rely entirely on the first. It would not be possible to educate intellectually without developing the language forms necessary to those skills studied. Learning and language benefit if the two processes are considered together. It should be possible to consider the entire language environment of the school, including the letters to parents, the circulars, and the notice boards. Even more important are the ways in which children are talked to in formal and informal situations, in playground, corridor, and assembly. It should then be possible to start monitoring, as Douglas Barnes suggests in Chapter 5, and then adjusting and teaching simultaneously. If the pupil is to grow intellectually, emotionally, and socially, he must feel at home in the school language environment. If this is to happen, that environment must not be too remote, and he must not be left unintroduced to it.

Teacher talk

At its worst the secondary classroom is mostly teacher talk: some figures show 70 per cent of the talk is by the teacher. Research in one case showed an average of one question every thirteen seconds! This gives barely time for a reply. Yet the voice of the teacher is not to be despised for that reason—it is one of the main modes of educating and there are other classrooms where it is heard too rarely. However, a whole-school language policy is likely to consider the use teachers make of their own talk. This will range from informal private chat on the one hand to careful exposition and reading aloud on the other. From another point of view it will range from communication with individuals, through small groups, full classes, and even such larger groupings as team-teaching gatherings, or school assemblies.

Such an enquiry is readily possible with the portable tape-recorder. The first step is to find out what is happening—that is, the proportion of one activity to another, and the extent of interaction with the pupils. The next step is to judge how well it is happening. It is rarely that any of us have had any attention paid to our own use of our voice from any point of view: indeed, it appears that most training courses give no specific tuition or consideration to teacher talk.

Considerable help is now available from Douglas Barnes, writing in the two books noted in the reading list, and later in this book he has contributed a consideration of how a school, a department, or a teacher can monitor success in communication. I should like to suggest here the various kinds of teacher talk that could be considered.[1]

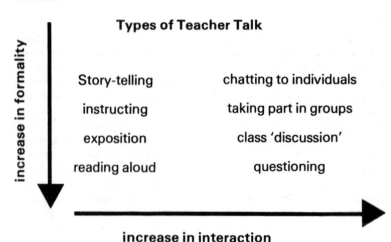

Types of Teacher Talk

increase in formality

Story-telling   chatting to individuals

instructing   taking part in groups

exposition   class 'discussion'

reading aloud   questioning

increase in interaction

In considering each type shown in the diagram, a policy is likely to give some advice based on group analysis of recordings of actual events. It will be seen that the teacher requires a flexibility to take him from his occasional role as 'performer' (most of the left-hand column have a performing aspect), to his person as, at one extreme, equal converser, and of course the more usual middle role of 'sympathetic adult'. It is fashionable now to play down the first. A science teacher, for instance, will insist that his subject works through small-group practicals, and he will refuse to believe he is ever a verbal performer. However, an observer will note full-class exposition, instructions, even reading aloud. The move to remind the teacher not to talk at the class the whole time must not mask the number of occasions when he must talk to them all, and talk well.

The art of giving a clear instruction, telling a vivid story (scientists, mathematicians, historians, and geographers all need to do this occasionally), and giving a clear exposition can be worked on. For instance, the sentence I quoted earlier as an instance of postponed meaning is an example of a common difficulty. In general, the pattern of a sentence should ensure that the point being made is emphasized by grammar, word order, and stress, so that the listener does not have to un-scramble, rearrange, and put together the elements of the remark before he can make sense of it. For instance, I once heard a

[1] I have also paid some attention to the *techniques* of instructions and questioning in *The Craft of the Classroom*, Heinemann Educational Books, 1975.